SpringerBriefs in Sociology

Series editor

Robert J. Johnson, University of Miami, Coral Gables, FL, USA

More information about this series at http://www.springer.com/series/10410

Tiffany Jones · Andrea del Pozo de Bolger
Tinashe Dune · Amy Lykins
Gail Hawkes

Female-to-Male (FtM) Transgender People's Experiences in Australia

A National Study

Springer

Tiffany Jones
School of Education
University of New England
Armidale, NSW
Australia

Amy Lykins
CBSS
University of New England
Armidale, NSW
Australia

Andrea del Pozo de Bolger
CBSS
University of New England
Armidale, NSW
Australia

Gail Hawkes
School of Arts
University of New England
Armidale, NSW
Australia

Tinashe Dune
Department of Health
University of New England
Armidale, NSW
Australia

ISSN 2212-6368 ISSN 2212-6376 (electronic)
SpringerBriefs in Sociology
ISBN 978-3-319-13828-2 ISBN 978-3-319-13829-9 (eBook)
DOI 10.1007/978-3-319-13829-9

Library of Congress Control Number: 2014958991

Springer Cham Heidelberg New York Dordrecht London

Printed on acid-free paper

Springer International Publishing AG Switzerland is part of Springer Science+Business Media (www.springer.com)

I would have been about four? I used to get really upset when in the mornings I'd check to see if I was a boy and wasn't. I'd then start my day upset and not understand why I wasn't a boy.

(Lance, male/transsexual male, 40 years)

... I feel male, but I feel like I can't call myself a man yet. After living as a female, I find it hard to deny the existence of a part of me that lived that. I don't really identify with the person I was, just the struggles I had. I believe my gender is evolving day by day and one day I will feel comfortable calling myself fully male... possibly after surgery. I had moments throughout my childhood where I knew. I had moments as a teen where I knew. But I suppressed it all. It all came crashing down around me when I was about 20. It happened when I saw the results of one guy's transition. I guess I didn't know that

transitioning was possible until then. I think that's why I suppressed it, because I didn't know there was an answer.

(Harry, FtM transgender, 24 years)

I identify as "Genderqueer" I like being visually ambiguous, but to friends who don't understand that concept I let them know I prefer masculine pronouns. "She" definitely makes me feel dysphoric.

(Hansel, genderqueer, age 22 years)

I went to four GPs (doctors) until I found one that would listen to me to my discussion. One GP said to me, "Why would you want to change your gender, you're such a pretty girl"! Disclosing something so personal to a stranger is a HUGE deal, and to be brushed of like that is just fucking bullshit.

(Fang, FtM transgender, 29 years)

Acknowledgments

The authors thank and acknowledge the University of New England's Faculty of Professions which contributed a grant towards this research, for the funding of this research. We also thank and acknowledge UNE Partnerships and the UNE School of Education who have contributed grants towards supporting Dr. Tiffany Jones and her work on this project.

Brian Landrigan has been an invaluable source of help with the development of the logo graphic for the project, the design of the website and other graphics and IT-related contributions. He also supported the team in an ongoing fashion throughout the project and was incredibly generous with his time and ideas. Dr. Anthony Marks kindly assisted with the development of the survey and questions. Dr. Mitra Rashidian also contributed some assistance in the early discussions about this project and forwarded on articles of interest to the *E-males* team.

The *E-males* project reference group guided the development of the questionnaire and the recruitment process. We thank all the members of this group for their commitment to this research, and also the members of UNE's GSMA, FtM Australia, the National LGBTIQ Health Alliance and the Freedom Centre, and a range of individuals who offered feedback and contributed ideas.

The research would not have been possible without the support of organisations, groups and individual activists all over Australia promoting the project by putting it into both professional and personal e-list mail-outs, placing advertisements on Facebook pages and websites, putting up posters in gender centres, including items in newsletters, and letting people know by word-of-mouth. These networks were the basis of the high number of participants and we owe them a real debt of gratitude. Here we particularly thank FtM Australia, FtM Shed, Transmen Australia, DUDE magazine, the National LGBTIQ Health Alliance, Ygender, the Zoe Belle Gender Centre, the "I'm Transgender Facebook" Page, Trans Health Australia, Transgender Victoria (TGV), Transgender Perth, Sydney Transgender International Film Festival, Male Trans Experiences Online, Trannyshack, GSMA, Australian Transgender Proud, Trans Panther SA, Freedom Centre WA, Australian Transsexuals, Transgender Support, Genderqueer Australia, the Transgender Studies Network, A Gender Agenda, The Pay-It-Forward Binder Program, PFLAG

Australia, Sally Goldner, Dani Wright, Sim Kennedy, GSAs and University-based support groups around Australia and many others.

We thank the GLBTIQ press who supported our work through reduced advertising rates, and generous interviews and stories on the research. We thank DUDE Magazine, LOTL Magazine, Sydney Star Observer, JOY 94.9 Melbourne (who gave us extensive interview time to promote the project and was a particular support) and all the other fantastic media serving our community. We also thank the mainstream press—including rural publications such as the Armidale Express—who not only promoted the recruitment drive for this project, but in doing so included interviews with Dr. Tiffany Jones that educated a broader Australian population about the many contributions transgender people make within the community.

Most importantly, we owe an extra special thanks to the Australians who took the time out of their day—sometimes briefly, sometimes over a period of weeks—to do the *E-males* survey and/or participate in the forum discussions. Your openness about yourselves, your experiences and your ideas for improving conditions were invaluable. Your contributions to research are greatly appreciated, and we hope this report will be a step towards supporting the many changes you would like to see in the future.

Contents

1 **Introduction** 1
Issues of (In)Visibility 1
Increased Policy Advocacy 2
Lack of Research 5
Research Frame and Aims 7

2 **Design of the Study** 17
Reference Group 17
Overall Approach 18
Data Collection Tools 18
The *E-Males* Survey 18
The *E-Males* Blog Forum 19
Terminology Use in the Study 19
Ethical Considerations 20
Sampling 21
E-Males Concept and Logo 21
Recruitment and Promotion 22
Press Release/Media 22
Internet, E-Lists, Networking 22
Social Networking Sites 23
Gender Centres 23
Data Analysis 24

3 **Our Diverse FtM Transgender Participants** 25
Key Findings 25
Number of Participants 26
How Participants Came to the Study 26
Age 26
State/Territory 27
Birth Sex 28
Gender Identity 29

Main Occupation 30
Birth Country 30
Ethnicity 30
Disability 31
Living Arrangements 31
Religion 31

4 **Gender Identity** 33
Key Findings 34
Self-Identification 34
Selection of Pseudonyms 34
Defining and Describing Gender Identity 36
Age of Discovery 38
Gender Identity Clinics 41

5 **Transitioning and Other Options** 45
Key Findings 46
Diverse Forms of Transitioning 46
Legal Transitions 48
Satisfaction with Transitioning 50
Impact on Wellbeing 51
Costs of Transitioning 53
Problems and Temptations 55

6 **Health** 57
Key Findings 58
Physical Health 58
Alcohol and Drug Use 59
Bad Experiences with Health Services 60
Good Experiences with Health Services 61
Other Lessons for Health Service-Providers 62

7 **Mental Health** 65
Key Findings 66
Life Satisfaction and Wellbeing 66
Mental Health Diagnoses 68
Self-harm 70
Suicide 72
Mental Health Services 73

8 **Education** 75
Key Findings 76
Education Level 76
Policy 78

Information Provision 79
Counselling 80
Uniforms 80
Bathrooms 81
Attitudes 82
Being Yourself at School 82
Ideas for Improvement 83

9 **Employment** 85
Key Findings 86
Employment Status 86
Income 86
Employment Obstacles 87
Employment Supports 89

10 **Discrimination, Social Acceptance and Support** 91
Key Findings 92
Discrimination 92
Coming Out 93
Being an Advocate 96
Going Stealth 97
Patterns in Social Life 98
Positive Experiences 100
Future Supports 101

11 **Sexuality, Romance and Relationships** 103
Key Findings 104
Relationship Status 104
Marital Status 105
Sexual Orientation 106
Sexual Identity 107
Impact on Sexual Life 109
Sexual Expressions 112
Sexual Protection 113

12 **Parenting** 115
Key Findings 116
Parenting and Identity 116
Becoming a Parent 116
Childless, Not Child-Free 118
Disclosure to Children 119

13 Conclusion and Recommendations 121
Trends and Individuals 121
Recommendations 122
Public Safety and Social Supports 122
Documentation 123
Education Policy 124
Employment Policy 125
Health and Medical Policy 125
Gender Identity Clinics, Experts and Services 126
Mental Health Services 126
Sexual Health Resources 127
Further Research 127
Future Advocacy 128
Conclusion 129

Appendix A: The Survey Questionnaire 131

Appendix B: The Forum Questionnaire 137

Glossary 143

References 149

Executive Summary

Introduction

This is the first national report on FtM transgender peoples' experiences in Australia. The FtM transgender people have been less "visible" in Australian culture and media in the past, compared to other people on the trans-spectrum. However, this is changing with a range of FtM transgender individuals featured in reality shows recently aired on Australian television. Increased advocacy in the last decade by both global and Australian networks has secured greater recognition of the right to non-discrimination on the basis of gender identity in international human rights law and Australia's national and state laws. There have also been significant developments around the classification of gender identity-based diagnoses, education and health-care policy, and recognition of gender in documentation. However, there has been a lack of research on transgender people both overseas and in Australia, and existing studies were typically conducted in medical environments, subsumed FtM trans-gender people into broader populations or focussed on MtF people.

Design

In 2013, the *E-males* study was launched to increase the visibility of (and meet the research gaps on) FtM transgender Australians and their needs, with a view to informing policy. The *E-males* project included two components. First, we used an anonymous online survey which gathered basic data, combining both quantitative and qualitative questions to enable people with diverse identities and experiences to engage with the topics. Second, we used an anonymous online discussion-board forum, which allowed the participants to engage in deeper discussions of broader themes with the research team and other respondents (using a pseudonym of their choice). This design allowed participants to give feedback on, and co-create the topics and questions—to increase their ownership of the project and how they were to be presented. Participants were recruited through a range of recruitment techniques, including paid advertising, support groups and services, Facebook posts, e-lists, media interviews and so on. The study's design and recruitment processes were informed by a reference group including a diverse range of FtM transgender Australian individuals, and feedback from key organisations.

Our Diverse Participants

In total, 273 FtM transgender people participated in the *E-males* project; the largest number of FtM people in an Australian study. Participants ranged in age from 16 to 64, with the average age 30.5. The participants came from all states of Australia, but were slightly more concentrated in Victoria and in urban areas than the broader population. They represented a range of culturally and linguistically diverse (CALD) backgrounds. Overall, 97 % of the participants were allocated a female sex at birth, 3 % intersex. In terms of gender identity, most participants identify as male, but other identities (such as FtM transgender, transsexual male, genderqueer and so on) were represented. The group mostly lived in stable situations with their loved ones, and were mostly working or studying. A large portion (86 %) had no religious affiliation.

Gender Identity

Most *E-males* participants (51 %) identified simply as "male". Some of these men occasionally referred to themselves as "Genderqueer" or "transgender" when in a GLBTIQ context. This group tended to have known their identity from a young age, and had struggled with the development of secondary sex characteristics during puberty. However, some were unsure about their identity until later in life, and simply felt they inexplicably *did not feel right*. Participants who mainly identified as either 'transgender', 'trans male', 'FTM' or 'male with transgender or transsexual background' explained that referring to themselves only as only as male would deny a part of themselves. 'Genderqueer' was the preferred way to self-identify for those who rejected pressures to fit into female–male binary model or stereotypes—either since they did not relate to or agree with the binary, or due to an uncertainty about gender. Reading post-structuralist feminist or Queer books, study and reflections on gender binaries were part of this latter group's path of discovery. The participants expressed strong negative feelings about being referred to by female pronouns, regardless of their diverse gender identities. Many had little or no engagement with gender centres, gender experts, doctors or counsellors with adequate training. There was a need for more standardisation and accessibility to gender identity services and information.

Transitioning

Transitioning could have any or all of personal/internal, social, legal and physical elements. In terms of physical transitions, non-surgical measures were the most common, and a strong majority had used binding and hormones (87 %). Most of the E-male participants (73 %) have had physical interventions to make their body look more masculine and 70 % intend to have additional modifications—chest surgeries were the most popular type. Almost half of the participants spent between $1000 and $10,000 in this process. The great majority (97 %) expressed that these interventions have made a difference to their life and the way they felt, even when surgical results were not optimal. Impacts included lowering anxiety and depression for some, helping with confidence and preventing self-hate. Most (79 %) stated that their level of satisfaction with the results of the interventions ranged between somewhat satisfied and very satisfied. There were some difficulties for participants when they sought to change their names and sex on documentation, and some had been refused or shamed in the process, despite its high importance to their lives. No participant reported having to use unapproved treatments or someone else's prescriptions. For those who had been tempted, safety concerns had prevented them from doing so. However, genderqueer and younger participants were more exposed to people wanting to order testosterone online or through a friend's prescription, out of desperation. These groups could find it difficult to get the treatments they needed when psychologists did not understand or support them.

Health

Participants mainly considered their physical health to have been good or very good in the past year.

Unfortunately, they reported that many of the health service-providers they had used, such as doctors, had a lack of knowledge about transgender issues. They told stories of practitioners who were so uninformed, and therefore shocked by the patient, that they were unable to successfully complete the appointment or could not treat the patient. There were also reports of doctors making offensive statements and misgendering patients. The participants found themselves having to "educate" their doctors a lot, and there was a unanimous agreement amongst participants about the need for healthcare practitioners to have greater education on transgender issues. There was a lack of availability and/or visibility of transgender healthcare services in rural areas, and some participants spoke of having to travel for 4.5 h to get to practitioners who did not treat them inappropriately. Respondents greatly valued healthcare providers who educated themselves on transgender issues, were friendly, treated them in accordance with their gender identity and went above and beyond to help them get the assistance from other services that they required. Some participants did not disclose their transgender identity to their healthcare providers.

Mental Health

Whilst most participants were satisfied with their lives in general, a very high proportion (69 %) had received a diagnosis of depression and anxiety within the previous 12 months. The survey data revealed that over 80 % of the participants had thought about self-harm or suicide. Over two thirds had self-harmed (68 %) and over one third (35 %) had attempted suicide. The group mostly attributed their very high rates of self-harm and suicide risk to their personal issues in regards to their trans* identity. They also cited other issues, and experiences of transphobia. On the discussion-board forum blogs, many of the participants partly related their mental health problems to gender dysphoria. They often related improvements in mental health to the process of coming out about their gender identity, and the process of transitioning. The participants had used psychologists, psychiatrists, counselling through sexual and mental health organisations, gender identity experts, special queer youth counsellors and emergency hotlines. For many FtM Australians, using mental health services for their gender issues or their mental health needs many times over was not optional, but a necessary requirement for a transition they wished to pursue. Experienced, affirming gender-focussed providers with streamlined processes, high knowledge and ongoing support were the most valued. Expensive and disinterested psychiatrists and service-providers that were unknowledgeable or judgemental, were considered the most problematic.

Education

A large portion (69 %) of *E-males* participants had a post-secondary qualification. This was a higher portion than the general Australian population, and general transgender populations represented in the Australian research literature. Conversely, 4 % had not completed secondary school and had only had a primary school education—twice the portion of the general Australian population. The data suggested that schools were a tougher place for FtM transgender people than post-secondary educational institutions (due to a lack of protective school-level policies against transphobia, a lack of unisex uniforms and bathrooms, and a lack of awareness amongst staff and students—including counsellors). It is likely that transphobic discrimination means that some FtM transgender people drop out of school or seek apprenticeships earlier; yet, on the other hand, transphobic attitudes in the workforce might be keeping FtM people in post-secondary education (universities, TAFEs and other institutions which have fewer gendered requirements than some schools or jobs) for longer. Some participants had cleverly contrived to better their circumstances (in relation to uniform or other themes) within the limited opportunities available to them at school. Whilst protections for FtM transgender people accessing government education services have increased nationally and at the state level very recently, these protections have not yet rolled out to a great extent yet in schools.

Employment

The majority of participants (58 %) were working (full-time, part-time or in an apprenticeship). However, 15 % were unemployed—a higher portion than in previous studies on broader populations. The qualitative data revealed there were clear obstacles to employment and promotion for FtM people. These included the fear of coming out as transgender, transphobia in the workspace and in recruitment, the desire to avoid work during transition, uncertainty around the need to reveal gender history in a job or police check applications and fear of exposure in certain environments. Some workplaces and industries were perceived as more supportive than others, and there were examples of workplaces (such as warehouses) with very transphobic masculine work cultures that had compromising impacts even on men who had fully transitioned and 'passed' as male. Leadership (supervisors, management and so on) had a pivotal role in whether workplaces were transphobic or supportive. The participants recounted both stories of atrocious leadership behaviours, where supervisors were themselves abusive or let transphobic abuse continue after it was reported; and stories of best-practice leadership behaviours where supervisors provided appropriate support and gave clear guidelines to facilitate good work cultures in a no-fuss manner.

Social Support

Some people had no experiences of discrimination on the basis of transphobia, others had experienced public humiliation and verbal and/or physical abuse. Coming out was fraught with difficulties including the weight of keeping a secret and the potential end of key relationships. Mostly, coming out was a positive experience in that it relieved self-doubt, helped others better understand trans-identity and supported transitions. Sometimes participants felt they had to be advocates for FtM transgender communities, other times they reported 'going stealth' for safety reasons or to more fully embody their gender identity. Respondents' general wellbeing and quality of life was significantly influenced by relationships with family, friends and intimate partners. Difficulties in key relationships created distrust of others, support from these relationships seemed to increase general happiness. Positive social experiences were the result of accepting and non-judgemental family members, friends, queer peers, health professionals, colleagues and institutions.

Sexuality and Romance

Over half of the participants were in a romantic/sexual relationship. Most had never married. More than one third of the *E-males* participants were attracted to both sexes and a quarter were attracted to people of the opposite sex. Many were attracted to all gender expressions. Others were mostly driven towards femininity or masculinity as desirable attributes regardless of the person's sex. Others expressed that their sexual orientation fluctuated. Some of those who were 'lesbian' prior to transition, continued to be attracted to women but referred to themselves as 'straight men' post-transition. Some transgender men were comfortable with a wide variety of sexual behaviours. For some, being transgender had created self-doubt about how to proceed in sexual relationships. Others found that with the commencement of medical transition, they became more sexually active due to the way hormone therapy increased their libido and due to a greater comfort with their more masculine-looking bodies. FtM transgender people reported that they engaged in unpredictable variations on a broad range of sexual behaviours of varying risk (from kissing and giving oral sex using latex protections, through to receiving penetrative anal and vaginal sex without protection). This meant their sexual health risks were unpredictable, and there was a need for tailored information.

Parenting

Some of the *E-males* participants were parents and knew of other FtM parents. They expressed frustration that other people often do not recognise this fact, as for such respondents being a parent or father was an important element in their identity. FtM transgender people had become parents in a variety of different ways: through having had their own biological children, through fostering and adoption, through their partners and so on. Some respondents who were not intending to have children had given serious consideration to egg donation, and others enjoyed having children in their lives through other means—including being uncles to nephews and nieces. The question of disclosure (or not) of one's trans* status to one's children was considered a challenging one to navigate by some participants, with significant pros and cons on both sides. There was a growing need for more resources in this area.

Recommendations

We urge all government offices (including Centrelink offices), Medicare offices, post offices, banks, educational institutions, legal offices, real estate agents, social services and other places where documentation is required (featuring name and sex) to familiarise staff with the national *Guidelines on the Recognition of Sex and Gender* (Australian Government, 2013), and to provide sensitivity training around these processes. We encourage lawyers and gender support workers to familiarise themselves with the new documentation guidelines. We recommend Australia introduces a national education policy on GLBTIQ issues, which includes guidelines around combatting transphobia and the practical issues of supporting transgender people's needs in education, to give specific guidelines around issues like information provision, uniforms and bathrooms and management plans. We recommend workplace equity training measures for employers and unions, and leadership from supervisors on issues of transphobia. We recommend more training in gender identity issues for a range of other medical and health practitioners who may engage with FtM transgender Australians on various gender affirmation journeys (which may or may not include medical treatments). We highlight the need for consistency in provisions regardless of state, and the need for clearer standards based on research. Particular provisions for youth, genderqueer people and rural people are called for. Areas for further investigation that emerged from this study and areas of future advocacy are detailed.

Chapter 1
Introduction

Abstract This chapter introduces the first national study on Australian FtM transgender peoples' experiences. It argues that whilst FtM transgender people have been less "visible" in Australian culture and media in the past, this is changing with the advent of recent reality shows and websites. It discusses how increased advocacy in the last decade has secured greater recognition of the right to non-discrimination on the basis of gender identity in international human rights law and local Australian laws, and significant developments around the classification of gender identity-based diagnoses. Nevertheless there is a lack of research on transgender people, and existing studies were typically conducted in medical environments, subsumed FtM transgender people into broader populations or focussed on MtF people. The chapter outlines the theoretical frames used in such research, and explains the researchers' preference for a more post-modern framing that foregrounds the experiences of FtM transgender people in their own understandings.

Keywords Transgender · FtM · Visibility · Media · Rights · Law · Research · Theory · Studies · Post-modern

> I couldn't find any info when I was beginning my journey. The trans therapy/surgery circle is hard to discover without knowing someone who is in it. Even knowing whom the right therapists/surgeons are, you still can't discover any info about their work specific to the transsexual field (Harry, FtM transgender, 24 years).

Issues of (In)Visibility

FtM transgender people have been less "visible" in Australian culture and media in the past, even in comparison to other people on the trans-spectrum. Possible reasons include a difference in the physical visibility of Australian masculinities compared to femininities generally, and the different cultures around these identities. There has been a certain entertainment culture focussed more squarely on MtF identities

T. Jones et al., *Female-to-Male (FtM) Transgender People's Experiences in Australia*, SpringerBriefs in Sociology, DOI 10.1007/978-3-319-13829-9_1

embraced in Australian cabaret and cinema—prime examples included in the long-running *Les Girls and Carlotta* shows in Sydney's Kings Cross and the film *Priscilla* (which was referenced in the Sydney 2000 Olympic opening ceremony). In addition, some FtMs have simply desired to integrate/pass unnoticed within the category of their male gender, some have desired privacy around their gender histories, many have had genuine safety or practical employment discrimination concerns that may have tempered any wish to discuss their identity widely and so on. Yet the relative community-wide invisibility has been a double-edged sword. To some extent it protected the FtM community from the level of negative stereotyping that MtF Transgender people have experienced in public representations, the media and language historically. However, it has meant that some individuals' needs or desires for role models, community connections, and social advocacy at times went unmet. In addition, the celebration of the spectrum of FtM identities and the many positive experiences FtM people can have, has certainly been underdone.

The past decade has however seen an increasing level of visibility specifically for FtM people, particularly online. For example in 2001, the FTM Australia website was formed by two NSW men to provide quality information and support for men who transitioned FtM in Australia (http://www.ftmaustralia.org/). They also formed a meeting group and network, disseminated resources and have continually integrated new stakeholders as contributors and advisors. A range of Facebook and Twitter pages and groups, both open and closed, have been developed to support both online and offline discussions and events. Individuals have also created their own blogs, video logs and channels on YouTube to document and share their experiences of gender identity, transition impacts and so on. In addition, the last few years have also seen an increasing level of visibility for FtM identities on Australian TV Shows and media. For example, the singer Paige Elliot Phoenix famously discussed his gender history on the *X Factor* (2011), when asked why he had not auditioned in previous years. Local men and trans men have also featured on shows like *The Hungry Beast* (2011), and ABC2 has aired shows such as *My Transsexual Summer* (2012, 2013), *The Boy who was Born A Girl* (2012, 2013), *Head First: The Wrong Body* (2013) and others. New publications such as the Australian resource *DUDE Magazine,* which embraces a diverse range of FtM experiences and masculinities, have also gathered a strong following. Mainstream newspapers have featured a transsexual footballer and other stories (Stark 2009). Increased visibility has also stemmed from increased advocacy efforts more broadly across the GLBTIQ movement.

Increased Policy Advocacy

The last decade particularly has seen increased advocacy by global networks in relation to transgender issues and violence, education access, healthcare and medical treatments and social policy. In 2011 the United Nations Educational, Scientific and Cultural Organisation (UNESCO) held the First International Consultation on GLBTIQ issues in Educational Institutions in Rio de Janeiro, Brazil (December 6–9th). The event was attended by government and non-government representatives and education research experts on the topic from all continents (including the first author Dr Tiffany Jones), and they created the Rio Statement on the tenth International Human Rights Day (UNESCO 2011). The statement asserted that the right to education must not be 'curtailed by discrimination on the basis of sexual orientation or gender identity'. During the same period 200 UN Member States attended the New York convening 'Stop Bullying—Ending Violence and Discrimination Based on Sexual Orientation and Gender Identity'. The UN Secretary-General Ban Ki Moon contended bullying on these bases was "a grave violation to human rights and a public health crisis". This framing of human rights has subsequently been supported by the United Nations as a body, with the release of the United Nation's GLBTIQ-focussed *Born Free and Equal* policy (United Nations 2012). This document outlined the UN's position in interpreting GLBTIQ rights as inherent in 'human rights' for the first time, and asserted the protection of all people against discrimination on the basis of gender identity in international human rights law. It pushed for legislative protections and violence prevention measures in all nations.

During this period there were also heated debates over whether transgender identity issues really should be seen as a psychological disease or disorder, as they have been treated historically within earlier versions of the Diagnostical Statistics Manual (DSM)—used to diagnose and treat psychological conditions. Drescher (2002) recounted many gender diagnosis controversies during his tenure at the DSM-5 Workgroup on Sexual and Gender Identity Disorders and the ICD-11 Working Group on the Classification of Sexual Disorders and Sexual Health. During this period some activists pointed to how the previous removal of homosexuality from the manual had been a positive step against homophobia in the past, and were of the opinion that retaining notions of transgender issues as a psychological problem was pathologising. Drescher explained that ultimately the decision was made to enable transgender people to maintain access to care through maintaining the construction of gender identity as a psychological/medical issue requiring diagnosis. However, in the DSM-5 the diagnoses was changed from Gender Identity Disorder to Gender Dysphoria, and it was no longer bundled with the Paraphilias and Sexual Dysfunction section but given its own chapter within the manual to reduce stigma. The addition of a post-transition specifier was to be used in the context of continuing treatment procedures that serve to support the new gender assignment (a kind of "exit clause" from the diagnosis, which reduces stigma, when the post-transition individual is no longer gender dysphoric but still requires access to ongoing hormone treatment).

These international rights advocacy movements have certainly reinforced progress towards recognition of transgender rights in the Australian context, alongside the work of the Australian Human Rights Commission, and the sustained long-term efforts of local transgender advocacy groups and their allies. In June 2013 the Sex Discrimination Amendment (Sexual Orientation, Gender Identity and Intersex Status) Act 2013 (Cth) (SDA Amendment Act) inserted new grounds into the Sex

Discrimination Act 1984 (Cth) (SDA), particularly protections against discrimination for all Australians on the basis of gender identity. In the law 'gender identity' was defined as the gender-related identity, appearance or mannerisms or other gender-related characteristics of a person (s 4(1)). This included the way people express or present their gender and recognises that a person's gender identity may be an identity other than male or female. Notably, the direct use of labels such as transgender in the law were specifically avoided for fear they might be "offensive or inaccurate" (Australian Bureau of Statistics 2012c, p. 3). However it was intended to cover these identities and more, which we advocated for in its development (Jones 2012b, 2013a). The SDA provides protection from discrimination for people who identify as men, women, and neither male nor female. It does not matter what sex the person was assigned at birth, or whether the person has undergone any medical intervention. All states and territories had previously prohibited discrimination on some basis related to transgender issues. However, these grounds differed, having included: gender identity (ACT Parliamentary Counsel 2010; QLD Parliamentary Counsel 2010; VIC Parliamentary Counsel 2010); transsexuality (NT Parliamentary Counsel 2010; TAS Parliamentary Counsel 2010); transgender status (NSW Parliamentary Counsel 2010); chosen gender (SA Parliamentary Council 2010), or gender history (WA Parliamentary Counsel 2010).

The Australian Government is now seeking to address disparities in other state and territory laws around transgender rights through its newly released *Guidelines on the Recognition of Sex and Gender* (Australian Government 2013). Australia's first official "legal transsexual" transitioned legally through an amended birth certificate with the Births, Deaths and Marriages Department of NSW in 1987; and all Australian jurisdictions have since recognised the affirmed sex of an individual after surgery unless the person was married. However, there have been disparate requirements around surgery and sterility for recognition, which the new guidelines (to be implemented within three years) address. The guidelines support individuals to consistently identify and be recognised within the community as a gender other than the sex or gender they were assigned at birth, as intersex, or as an indeterminate sex and/or gender in their personal records. Where a person requests the sex and/or gender information on their personal record be amended, the Australian Government will now recognise any one of the following as sufficient evidence regarding sex/gender:

(a) a statement from a Registered Medical Practitioner or a Registered Psychologist,
(b) valid Australian Government travel document, such as a Valid Passport, which specifies their preferred gender, or
(c) an amended State or Territory birth certificate, which specifies their preferred gender. A State or Territory Gender Recognition Certificate or recognised details certificate showing a State or Territory Registrar of Birth Deaths and Marriages has accepted a change in sex will also be seen as sufficient evidence (Australian Government 2013).

Sex reassignment surgery and/or hormone therapy are not pre-requisites for the recognition of a change of gender in Australian Government records, or in passports. Similarly, under the Australian passport policy for applicants who are sex and gender diverse, a letter from a medical practitioner certifying that the person has had, or is receiving, appropriate clinical treatment for gender transition to a new gender, is acceptable evidence of gender identity. A passport may be issued to intersex, transgender and/or gender diverse applicants in M (male), F (female) or X (indeterminate/unspecified/intersex) (www.passports.gov.au/web/sexgenderapplicants.aspx). Subsequent changes to align Medicare policies with this broader recognition of transgender people have been announced, so that transgender people will face less discrimination around healthcare benefits (Plibersek and McLucas 2013).

Australia has also increasingly seen decisions by Family Courts supporting transgender children to start puberty blockers at younger ages such as 11/12 years old (Fewster 2013; McCredie 2008), or supporting transgender adolescents to receive surgical procedures towards transition (Kissane 2009). There was some controversy over the recent decision by a Family Court in NSW to allow an orphaned FtM transgender child to take puberty blockers with the support of his foster parents, and the rejection of the idea that a Family Court would even be necessary to approve the treatment in the future (Miletic and Browne 2013). Some conservative religious groups, and a few individual academics known for their previous attacks on transgender childrens' rights such as Sheila Jeffreys (Karvelas 2013; Miletic and Browne 2013; Robotham 2012), were outraged at the state's support for the boy's self-definition—framing treatments for gender dysphoria as so-called "child abuse" and even attempting to denounce the inclusion of gender identity as a ground in anti-discrimination law. However, we note that Jeffreys is a radical feminist focussed on a cissexist view of womens' rights, who has never researched or worked with gender questioning youth or transgender adults. Transgender rights groups and GLBTIQ people, and direct researchers of transphobia and transgender issues (including ourselves and researchers from a Melbourne-based university clinic), have largely applauded the changes in the Australian context as positive steps (Miletic and Browne 2013; Transgender Victoria et al. 2013).

Lack of Research

When preparing a Massive Online Open Course on Prejudice and Discrimination, we were frustrated by the dearth of research on transgender people. There was certainly work on "transgender" as a concept; with some theorists framing it as related to intersex elements within brain composition, some as a gender issue that is sociological and distinct from physical chemistries, some as a deconstruction of gender, some as problematic according to conservative or radical feminist critique. There were varied frames including biological science/chemistry/biology, sociology, feminism(s), medical science (the limits and possibilities of medical treatment),

Queer theory, psychology and many others influencing the field. However work which gives transgender people themselves ***an actual voice*** in such matters is alarmingly rare.

Worldwide the research has focussed more strongly on male-to-female (MtF) transgender people, has typically been conducted in medical environments (gender clinics, sexual health centres, hospitals), and for small sample sizes. Topics explored have included HIV risk and sexual health (Clements-Nolle et al. 2001; Edwards et al. 2007), sex reassignment surgery (De Cuypere et al. 2005; Lawrence 2005; Rehman et al. 1999), and mental health (Clements-Nolle et al. 2006; Grossman and D'Augelli 2006, 2007; Haraldsen and Dahl 2000; Hepp et al. 2005). Research with a social focus has been certainly less common, and thus many aspects of transgender experience have been overlooked. However, there have been a few studies that have considered transgender and gender questioning youths' experiences of school bullying (Kosciw et al. 2010; Russell et al. 2011) and family rejection (Grossman et al. 2005, 2006). Occasionally national studies on students generally have included a single question on gender identity—for example in New Zealand, where 1 % of students reported that they were transgender (including culturally specific identities such as Fa'afafine, Whakawāhine, Tangata ira Tane) and an additional 3 % were questioning their gender/unsure (Clark et al. 2013).

Internationally, research into the history of FtM people in both ancient and modern times has been difficult. This has been in part due to sexism and the ways in which the lives of female-bodied people have been less recorded throughout time than those "of men" (Devor 1997), in part due the shame and subsequent disassociation by early 20th century doctors engaged in sex re-assignment surgeries with the procedures they performed (Halberstam 1998), and in part due to social resistance to the concept that men (considered the "original" gender) could be constructed compared to women (whose gender was more readily accepted as socially created) (Tiernan 2009). There has been some rather ambiguous coverage of FtM transgender people undergoing perceived sex changes in the journal *Urania* in the 1930s—such as a Margaret Hutchinsen who entered a hospital as a girl and left as a boy in an article entitled "Another Change of Sex" (Tiernan 2009). There was also information uncovered by historians on Michael Dillon (born 1915), a medical studies graduate who had undergone various sex reassignment procedures in the 1940s (Kennedy 2006).

There has been limited research on Australian transgender people. Recent studies have mainly focussed on a broader Australian Transgender population (Collyer and Heal 2002; Couch et al. 2007; Pitts et al. 2006), or broader GLBTIQ population (Hillier et al. 2010; Jones 2012c; Pitts et al. 2006). *Tranznation* (Couch et al. 2007; Pitts et al. 2006) focused on a sample of 253 Australian and New Zealand sample of FtM and MtF transgender people, with only 229 Australians and only a third of the portion for FtM transgender people as there were MtFs represented. Its findings revealed that the most commonly accessed health service by transgender people was mental health. Three quarters of the sample had accessed hormonal treatment and most of the sample had not received any surgical procedure. Surgery was shown to increase general satisfaction, despite associated pain and complications. Most of the sample had suffered stigma or discrimination on the basis of gender.

Writing Themselves in 3 (Hillier et al. 2010) included a sample of 91 gender questioning youth aged 14–21, within a broader group of 3,134 same sex attracted and gender questioning youth. The gender questioning youth were found to be more likely to be out than same-sex attracted youth but let less likely to get support from the people they disclosed their identities to, and were more likely to have dropped out of or moved schools as a result of discrimination (Jones and Hillier 2013). They were also at greater risk of homelessness, physical abuse, self-harm and suicide. However, they had higher engagement with activism against homophobia and transphobia, particularly in their schools (Jones and Hillier 2013).

Most studies focussed exclusively on female-to-male (FtM) samples came from North America (Barrett 1998; Newfield et al. 2006; Pazos 2000; Yerke and Mitchell 2011). Barrett (1998) discussed the disappointment that could occur with the surgeries available at the time, however there have been developments in procedures and skill over time that have not yet been explored exclusively for FtM transgender people in Australia. Newfield et al. (2006) discussed quality of life factors, but these could be very different for the Australian context. Pazos (2000) reflected on counselling experiences with several of her FtM clients, and noted the recurrence of feelings of difference as early as five years of age, magical thinking and daydreaming about becoming a boy, and early attempts at "making the change" through trying to urinate standing up and engaging in attempts to look or act like boys. Risk of STD and HIV infection was seen as high in some American contexts such as San Francisco and other areas, due to the high risk sexual behaviours FtM people there engaged in (Kenagy and Hsieh 2005; Rowniak et al. 2011; Stephens et al. 2011). Hyper sexuality and genital changes (dryness, which created bleeding during intercourse) from hormone therapy, the unfamiliar nature of the gay community for men who had sex with men, and incorrect assumptions concerning risk were factors. In response to these issues, we wanted to explore how FtM Australians engaged in, and protected themselves during, sexual engagements with others. Yerke and Mitchell (2011) showed that a group of FtM transgendered individuals who transitioned 20 years beforehand were much more likely to go through hormonal treatment and complete surgery procedures, whereas now trends have shifted so that a group who had transitioned more recently were more likely to only access hormonal treatment and top surgery (and did not see bottom surgery as an essential part of transition). The *E-males* research team therefore wanted to address the current gap in Australian research on the specific experiences and beliefs about transition for contemporary Australian FtM transgender people.

Research Frame and Aims

There are different groups of theorists with investments in FtM transgender identities. Often those investments are conflicting. Debates can break out amongst scholars in academic texts and conferences over the particulars of ideas that, frankly, may at first seem to have little to do with the lived experiences of FtM people themselves. A very brief history of the conceptualisation of FtM people in theory will aid understanding of these debates, and why we took the position we did in this research.

FtM transgender variance and cross-dressing before the 19th century was not always read in relation to identity in European theory, but in relation to female violation of social roles and marital ritual (Foucault 1980; Garber 1992). By the end of the 19th century masculinity in female-bodied people was associated in a Freudian psycho-analytic frame with the psychological disorder of "inversion" (which combined early concepts of lesbianism, role confusion and penis envy), and with feminist preoccupations (Chauncey 1989; Freud 1905). "Masculine women" generally became associated in psychoanalysis and sexology with aberrant sexual desire emanating from severe cross-gender identification, and were cast by conservatives and traditionalists as a sign of the "ills of modern life"—a coarsening of females, loss of separation of gender spheres and family structures, and degeneration of the species (Halberstam 2012). During World War 1 these anxieties were furthered as women took over "male" factory jobs and domestic tasks. Jewish theorist Otto Weininger's rather misogynistic work was used to negate the growing push for women's rights and to incorporate sexologists' understandings of inversion. He had argued that the social, political and aesthetic desires of women for liberation were innate for those great achievers (Sappho, Catherine the Great) whom he deemed virtual men; but only falsely acquired by women who associated with them. He pushed for the liberation of the "invert" who was psychically male and physically fit to undertake male jobs, but conversely pushed against the broader women's movement and saw the rightful place of "feminine" women to be at home (Weininger 1906).

Perhaps understandably, many liberal feminists in the 1960s pushed back against such thinking about political women as "manly", because it functioned to limit their rights (Tuttle 1986). But this unfortunately meant they increasingly saw accusations of inversion, lesbianism or "women becoming men" as a threat to their political equality. This created tensions with the transgender, and gay and lesbian communities who had often shared spaces (street protests, campaigns) with heterosexual female feminists. From the 70s some extremist radical feminists went even further in specifically excluding transgender people only, by delineating female identities from masculinity and transgender people in theory, and creating womyn-only spaces (camps, bars) and privileging women-only (political and non-penetrative, lesbian) sexualities in practice. Janice Raymond's bitingly transphobic work then and now framed transsexuals as using medical technologies to invade women's spaces and bodies (Raymond 1994), Sheila Jeffrey's patronising treatments then and now framed transgender people as "mutilated" victims of patriarchy who reproduced its gender roles (Jeffreys 1994; Tuttle 1986). Post-modern and post-structuralist feminisms from the 80s influenced by (the now transitioned) Patrick Califia, and Queer theory popularised in the 90s by Judith Butler, do not declare such enmity with FtM transgender people or butch lesbians (Butler 1990, 2004; Califia 1981). These frames instead attack essentialist notions of identity (male, female, gay, straight, or otherwise), positing gender as discursive (culturally constructed), although they sometimes lack focus on embodiment and material experience. Transgender studies, kick-started by Sandy Stone's *The Empire Strikes Back* (Stone 1991), aims at affirming self-definition and the right to positive representation (mainly in self-reflection, media representations and literature). There are also currently frames based on brain sex which theorise FtM transgender people as having had brain areas develop as "chemically male" through hormonal exposure in the womb (Pease and Pease 2003). It is important to note that all these new frames do not simply "replace" older ones, but co-exist in tension with them and each-other, along with residual psychological frames re-shaping inversion into newer concepts of Gender Identity Disorder/GID, and more recently gender dysphoria.

Table 1.1 provides a comprehensive overview of the dominant discourses on FtM transgender issues in the literature. In this framework we have classified these paradigms as conservative, liberal, critical or post-modern in orientation; borrowing from a framing of discourses as having an overall function in social systems towards or against the maintenance of dominant existing social power structures and social orders (Jones 2013c). As argued elsewhere in relation to methodological frames of sexuality education research, GLBTIQ identities are similarly used in research studies in ways which reflect or disrupt social orders (Jones 2013b). For brevity's sake the table here does not include all possible perspectives on FtM transgender people; we particularly exclude many culturally-specific views which did not usefully apply to the Australian data presented in this book (e.g. "Bacha Posh" practices where some daughters in Afghanistan and Pakistan are raised boys for reasons of inheritance or financial support, see Ehrensaft 2011). The table allows comparison of the different views of FtM transgender people and the discourses from which they derive. It allows us to organise our main objections to these perspectives, to clarify our rationale for why the majority do not serve as our analytic frame. The conservative discourses could not drive our analyses because they function overall to keep FtM transgender people (and others who do not fit in with their particular privileged identity ideals of cisgender heterosexual males and females) at the bottom of restrictive notions of the social order. For example, conservative religious frames may endorse closeted or repressed FtM transgender people who do not enact their desired identities (perhaps supporting the idea that they will be spiritually rewarded for this repression and suffering in a discursively specific afterlife), however they propound a damnation of FtM transgender people who do enact their identities whilst also erasing their identity claims (positioning them as errant females) (Gahan and Jones 2013; Gahan et al. 2014). Biological essentialism does not recognise FtM identities as "real" but as aberrations; females undergoing confusion or inadequacies in their sex role development (Heilmann 2011). Psychiatric/psycho-analytic frames can be useful towards enabling medical transitions and allowing treatment of any related conditions of depression (Drescher 2013), but have a pathologising history with a residual social impact, and largely problematise the internal FtM experience to a degree (as a disorder, dysphoric). Political Essentialism (e.g. Weininger's work) includes Psychological males in male privileges equitably, but only perceives equal rights as the domain of "men" generally, overlooking the rights of women, gender diverse and intersex people.

Table 1.1 Dominant discourses on FtM transgender people in the literature

Theoretical orientation	Dominant discourses	FtM trans identity position/s supported
Conservative: reinforces the dominance of status quo identities through institutional powers, traditions and practices	*Conservative religious frames (particularly in Islamic/ Judeo-Christian traditions)* reinforce the centrally-determined norms of religious identities (male dominance and female subservience, marriage as a structure sanctioned by god as the sole site for sex as procreation, traditional families) via their leaders, spiritual texts and churches	Deviant/sinner/errant woman (as opposed to normatively gendered women and men)
	Biological essentialism sees males as biologically pre-destined to be masculine and females as biologically pre-destined to be feminine, towards the purpose of reproduction of set social orders and the human species, based on an overly basic biology and reading of Darwinian principals	Aberrant developments which do not aid the reproduction of the species (as opposed to the biologically normative and reproductively "successful" cisgender individual)
	Psychological frames analyse disruptions to, and reinforcing, psychological health through corrective clinical practices	Inversion, GID, gender dysphoria (as opposed to the psychologically healthy cisgender individual)
	Political biological essentialism explains "great women" who are high achievers in traditionally "masculine realms" (politics, work, sports) as basically (and equal to) men	The psychological/political male (as opposed to feminine women)
Liberal: makes accessible through minor reforms to existing systems the liberties and freedoms of individual identities	*Liberal biological/medical sciences (brain sex frames)* recognise the biological diversity within the human species in the combinations of chromosomes (XX/XY/ XXY), hormones, androgyns and their impacts on brains/ bodies	Pre-op and post-op patients generally requiring hormonal/ surgical corrections or maintenance to redress mind-body incongruences (as opposed to the more common healthy cisgender individual)

(continued)

Table 1.1 (continued)

Theoretical orientation	Dominant discourses	FtM trans identity position/s supported
	Liberal feminisms reinforce through minor reforms (within current systems) the liberties and freedoms of women. Some liberal feminists pushed back against the view of political women as "manly", because it limited the rights of women broadly	Masculine women, and FtM people, can be rejected in some versions
Critical: pushes for whole-scale reforms of existing systems in the interest of a marginalised group	*Radical feminisms* push for whole-scale reforms and alternate segregationist spaces in the interests of women	Mutilated victims of patriarchy who reproduced its gender roles, in attempts to invade sex-segregated spaces
	Gay liberationisms push for whole-scale reforms and alternate segregationist spaces in the interests of gay people, and these days the GLBTIQ (gay, lesbian, bisexual, transgender, intersex and queer)/LGBT umbrella	Part of the GLBTIQ/LGBT umbrella of identities to be advocated for
	Transgender studies push for whole-scale reforms and alternate segregationist spaces (particularly in theory work, but also in activism) in the interests of transgender people	FtM transgender, transman, trans*, bois and other terms from trans-specific cultures and writings (as opposed to cisgender groups)
Post-modern: questions the norms of status quo, grand narratives, existing systems and identities themselves	*Post-modern/post-structural feminisms* posit that in hegemonic narratives of gender, binary oppositions between sex, gender and sexuality uphold ideals of certain masculine male and feminine female identities as oppositional above and beyond other potential variations	A range of masculinities and femininities, on a range of bodies, are accepted and pointed out to disrupt gender norms
	Queer theory argues all identity is an inauthentic cultural creation, regardless of the body on which it is enacted. The illusion of authenticity relies on the stabilising structures of binary	FtMs subvert/reveal the inauthenticity of maleness through their re-appropriated gender performativity, but are no less or more "real males" than those declared male at birth. Genderqueer identities

(continued)

Table 1.1 (continued)

Theoretical orientation	Dominant discourses	FtM trans identity position/s supported
	oppositions between sex, gender and sexuality which uphold masculine male heterosexual and feminine female heterosexual identities as oppositional norms beyond which all else is negated	declare upfront one's gender identity is inconsistent, fluid or somehow alternative to established norms
	Post-modern relativism posits that in hegemonic narratives of gender, binary oppositions between sex, gender and sexuality uphold ideals of certain masculine male and feminine female identities as oppositional above and beyond other potential variations, however these other identity construction variations can be experienced equally as truths by those who inhabit them	Acknowledges any of the identities used in the experience of the individuals/ groups under exploration, including those listed above as relevant, rather than asserting universal identity category 'truths'

* Broad coverage of a range of transgender identities

The liberal discourses were not placed at the core of our analyses because they problematised FtM transgender identities overall, even though they did so in support of particular individuals' access to rights and resources. Liberal biological/ medical/neurological sciences (brain sex frames) can be useful for enabling access to medical transitions and resources, but some FtMs eschew medical transitions/ "corrections" for financial, political, medical or other reasons and do not see themselves within "pre-op/post-op" or "patient" conceptualisations (Roen 2001, 2011). Liberal feminisms, in seeing women as equal to men and focusing on their access to male-dominated domains, overlook FtM people's particular needs and may even actively create distance from views of women as "manly" (a common attack) to aid the cause (Tuttle 1986). Some of the critical discourses on the other hand were potentially suitable in their push for more whole-scale reform—although clearly radical feminisms (particularly the extreme work mentioned earlier) can potentially victimize and erase transgender people in their essentialist efforts to differentiate women from men. Gay liberationist discourse can borrow on the political successes of gay activisms to push forward FtM transgender peoples' rights concomitantly (Byne 2014), but as a small sub-group within the GLBTIQ umbrella the specific needs of people with FtM transgender identities can be overlooked, particularly where hierarchies of power (race/gender/cissexism) exist within GLBTIQ activisms causing them to focus mainly on the interests of white gay men for example (Stryker 2008). Transgender studies (built on the work of Stone and other transgender activists) was the most useful of the critical approaches in acknowledging a range of transgender experiences in the frames in which transgender people experience, embody and voice them (Nagoshi and Brzury 2010); and we took this acknowledgement of self-definition and narratives into our study. However we did not rely exclusively on this perspective due to its main usefulness in enabling transgender people to speak for themselves *to themselves*, and our wish to make this data accessible to a range of interested policy makers, sociologists and other academics, and allies in addition to transgender readers. In the liberal and critical views there is tendency to absolutise differences between insiders and outsiders in this way (Young 1997). A relativism is adopted in which each individual's view (liberal), or each group's culture (critical) is true or valid in its own right but strictly or largely incommensurable with the understandings of others and outsiders (Bhabha 1990; Jones 2013c; Young 1997). We felt the need to mediate this tendency.

We found the more inclusive post-modern approaches best suited to our study, including the manner in which they questioned the norms of status quo, grand narratives and identities themselves (Lankshear and Knobel 2000; Lyotard 1984). Although transgender issues were not the main focus of post-structuralist feminisms, they were more central to Queer theory. Elements of this approach we used included the acknowledgement of queer and genderqueer as alternative positions disrupting mainstream sexualities and gender identities. However, we note that using Queer frames overly much can be problematic to a degree in their tendency to over-theorise (other peoples') lived experiences in set vocabularies (Butler 1990, 2005) which question the authenticity claims of the identities participants (or the groups under discussion) declare. Whilst Queer allows a kind of relative authenticity to FtM identities—in that a "male identity" is seen as no more authentic when enacted by one who was declared male at birth as by one who was not, the authenticity allowed is in a non-essentialist frame. In this theory states of female and male are not recognized as "truths", and gender is understood as performatively constructed through iterations and repetitions of culturally established behaviours, mannerisms and so on. Embodied experiences can therefore be overlooked (Nagoshi and Brzury 2010), and this is really an anti-identity framework which in its disruptive nature can actually upset those who have long struggled to claim a "true male core" or other core self for example. Ultimately, we realize that whether or not our participants' gender is "real" or cultural, biologically and/or socially determined, or otherwise in our view does not really matter—the aim of our research is to understand how they themselves experience it rather than to take their understandings and twist them into alternative models of our own preferences.

Given the contrasting theories around whether FtM transgender identities are linked to brain chemistries or cultural context, and given that FtM transgender people may themselves see their identities in queer, psychiatric, medical, biological or other terms (in their self-definition), we were careful to keep this project "open" to diversity. We took a Post-modern Relativist view of "FtM transgender" as a fractured and discursively contested/constructed umbrella term, associated with a range of identities. We accepted that it had multiple meanings to multiple people (who experience or research it according to their particular framework/s of reference, and therefore understand it within their framework). We used this broad frame so as not to limit the data, or exclude people with variant experiences to a more "stable" version of the term. Post-modernism had a strong emergence in the 1980s, and stems from the critique of French intellectuals around grand narratives[1] during the 1960s and 1970s, which swiftly spread to academics internationally (Carlson 2005; Leitch et al. 2001). Especially in Foucault's work (1969, 1970, 1976, 1979, 1980), post-modernism makes evident connections with mainstream social science, the sociology of power and the study of sexual and gender identities. The theory behind this study is located in a post-modern and somewhat post-structural paradigm; with Queer and Trasngender Studies aspects. It rejects the notion of a singular grand meta-narrative of Australian FtM transgender identity (Lyotard 1984, p. xxii) and considers its 'truths', along with deconstruction of the vocabularies, grammar and structures of the discursive field in a post-structuralist fashion (Leitch et al. 2001, p. 21). It takes an oppositional relation to the dominant order of the 'real', allowing recognition of all identity positions' partialities, in the spirit of Morton and Zavarzadeh's 'incompleteness and committedness' (1991, p. 12). It also applies Queer's interest in (de)constructions of sex and gender (Butler 1990; Jagose 1996), and Transgender Studies' interests narratives of self-definition, experience and embodiment (Nagoshi and Brzury 2010). Key post-modern aims include the demystification of 'hegemonic truths' (deep-seated cultural assumptions) and problematisation of knowledge. This position provides sufficient challenge to established social orders which exclude FtM transgender people, questioning the idea of norms in identity hierarchies, without disrupting the coherencies of individual identity as a user-experienced concept within its own narratives. It has the potential to acknowledge a great diversity of FtM transgender identities and experiences, without over-theorising the sense of their essentialism in some participants' lived experience (Hekman 1999, 2008). However, whilst we acknowledge that the "FtM transgender" marker is used by many people in many ways, we reject essentialist cissexist views of gender that don't allow for trans identities at all or cast them as "sinful", and extremist radical feminist notions of transgender people as "victims of patriarchy"—we instead accept that it is possible for transgender people to have empowered and positive experiences of transitions of various kinds, as well as to be gender non-conforming without seeking transition aids. In our analytical hierarchy, we privilege the self-definitions of those who apply the "FtM transgender" sign to themselves; for they are the ones who bring it to life in their varying embodiments of it, impact it most in their shifting materialist negotiations of it in different contexts and points in their lives, and expand its boundaries in their many subversions of it. We bring forth how these evaluate

[1] Overarching stories about history or reality based on universalist notions of truth, which overlook alternative perspectives.

vertically the value of religious, scientific, psychological, queer and other frames as they arise; without imposing external analyses.

Our view in that sense incorporates a degree of pragmatic pluralism—accepting that there are distinctions in how FtM transgender people view themselves or are viewed, but that these can (and do) speak to and influence each-other in practice to an extent, borrowing from and adjusting other vocabularies with overlapping terms, new concepts or resignified meanings (particularly around notions of gender identity and transition). Whilst there is no one truth to FtM transgender identities but many frames experienced as truths in a more pluralist manner, we do note where relevant the intercultural critiques that arise in the data (Young 1996). Post-modern relativism is more useful in dealing with differences within sub-cultures than in comparative work across several different ethnic cultures in this way (Young 1997). Thus we use pluralism not in the "vertical" sense (of treating questions as distinct in different domains of science, religion or the social for example), but in the "horizontal" sense (acknowledging that there can be more than one correct account of how things are in any one given domain—particularly across social identifications), to oppose the type of relativism that eschews hierarchies of domains of knowledge (Baghramian 2004). The main critique of the post-modern position is that it offers no solutions to 'real world' problems (Callewaert 2006; Frank 1989).[2] Manfred Frank provides the key neostructuralist critique of Foucault's assertion that there is nothing outside of discourse,[3] arguing that this critique suggests there is no true reality and offers only chaos (Frank 1989, pp. 183–184). Frank further contends that assembling orders of discourse (through analysis) is an attack on order that favours disorder, making post-modernists 'against everything' such that their critiques of dominant powers are valueless (Frank 1989, pp. 184–187). Yet such critique misunderstands that while post-modernism rejects a single 'true reality' beyond discourse, it doesn't theorise *any* exteriority to the discursive orders to constitute Frank's 'chaos'. In addition, while all discourses are indeed partial, some are nevertheless more useful (or less problematic) than others. The existing social orders of the discursive field are not conceived in this study as entirely extinguishable, but we certainly understand them as changeable. Thus, we believe directions for stakeholders around future re-ordering *can* have value and include recommendations in this book.

The research team therefore hoped to generate research that would encourage the general affirming spirit of recent critical changes in legislation and policy, with a focus on specifying any particular needs of FtM transgender people, as we have previously in the fields of health, education, and human rights legislation for gender questioning youth. We aimed to support the social justice interests of our research

---

[2] Examples of these problems (given in critique of the paradigm) are class- and sex-based struggles.

[3] Central to critiques reliant on universal structures, for example, Marxist and radical feminist criticisms.

participants, as well as their determination in their own cultural representation. This project was therefore conducted:

- towards visibility of FtM transgender people (but without the requirement of visibility/or 'outing' of individuals who participate);
- towards redressing research lacks for FtM transgender people; and
- towards informing future advocacy for FtM transgender people.

Chapter 2
Design of the Study

Abstract In 2013, the *E-males* study was launched to increase the visibility of (and meet the research gaps on) FtM transgender Australians and their needs, with a view to informing policy. This chapter describes the study's two design components: an anonymous online survey which gathered basic data through quantitative and qualitative questions, and an anonymous online discussion-board forum which facilitated deeper discussions of the key themes with the research team and other respondents. This design allowed participants to give feedback on, and co-create, the topics and questions—to increase their ownership of the project and how they were to be presented. Participants were recruited through a range of recruitment techniques, including paid advertising, support groups and services, Facebook posts, e-lists, media interviews and so on. The study's design and recruitment processes were informed by a reference group including a diverse range of FtM transgender Australian individuals, and feedback from key organisations.

Keywords Transgender · FtM · Research · Study · Methodology · Method · Internet · Survey · Blog · Forum

> I'm very open about it. I feel if people are willing to learn about gender identity, I'm willing to share what I know (Draconem, FtM transgender, 24 years).

Reference Group

In the past, FtM transgender Australians have been a difficult group to reach out to, due to issues of visibility and a lack of widely known social support groups and services. However the contemporary context facilitated several opportunities to reach out to people in this demographic, which the researchers were keen to take advantage of in order to develop the field. Opportunities to make contact abounded through the increased range of specifically FtM transgender focussed (and transgender and GLBTIQ) social groups, support groups, services and media. There were also prospects for making contact through new media technologies and social

T. Jones et al., *Female-to-Male (FtM) Transgender People's Experiences in Australia*, SpringerBriefs in Sociology, DOI 10.1007/978-3-319-13829-9_2

networking sites, advocacy networks, gender clinics and individual rights champions. To ensure that these opportunities were used respectfully, we formed a small informal reference group of individual representatives from the FtM transgender community who advised us on the name of the study, and the best and most respectful ways to proceed with various elements of the *E-males* project in their view.

Overall Approach

The research team used an emancipatory approach—aiming to conduct research on, with and for the FtM transgender community. We aimed to serve social justice goals for the community (rather than simply to generate knowledge for its own sake). The reference group was particularly helpful in discussing our initial ideas about what those goals might be. The project was particularly geared towards topics relevant to legislative and policy advocacy that have emerged locally and internationally in recent years, and envisioning service and resource needs for the community. In order to gather useful data for such ends, a mixed methods approach was used.

Data Collection Tools

A combination of an online survey and an online blog forum were used to collect the data. The survey questionnaire contained both forced-choice (quantitative) and open-ended (qualitative) questions.

The E-Males Survey

The survey was mainly used to gather basic descriptive data on the demographics, identities, and experiences of participants in relation to their gender identity. This tool was specifically designed to be completed in a short space of time—approximately 10–15 min. It was anonymous, and the responses were visible only to the participant and the researchers. The key topics explored in the survey included basic information such as age, background, life circumstances, employment status, identity and so on. Early drafts of the survey were reviewed by the reference group, members of key organisations embedded in the FtM community and contacts in our extensive transgender networks. The survey design is appended (Appendix A). The survey was hosted by UNE, using the program Qualtrics. It had a URL that included a university-based web address.

The E-Males Blog Forum

The blog forum was contrastingly used for deeper explorations of key themes over time, and for interactive engagement with the research team and other participants. This tool was specifically designed to be used and re-used for longer spaces of time as needed—completion times varied greatly. Dependent on the level of engagement with both the key research topics and the *E-males* blogging community a participant wished to have, a respondent could for example answer one question quickly and skip the others, respond to a few questions and suggest some extra ones, or perhaps answer all the topics extensively and come back to engage with other peoples' answers repeatedly throughout the duration of the study. The forum included a main section (for people over 18) and a separate section (for people aged 16–17). Several members of the team moderated and reviewed the posts on the forum daily, and where participants wanted a question included or revised in the study for example, any reasonable effort was made to adapt the study to the needs and visions of the participants to increase their ownership of the study, and to enhance control over their own representation.

The key topics explored further on the forum included gender identity, coming out, the impact of transitioning on wellbeing, sexuality, life satisfaction, health care, mental health, services, social inclusion, education, employment opportunities, community, legal issues and others. Early drafts of the forum were reviewed by the reference group, members of key organisations embedded in the FtM community and contacts in our extensive transgender networks. However, the forum was also modified in line with the suggestions of the forum participants themselves; one example of a theme that was added at the request of participants was the section on family/parenting. The forum design is appended (Appendix B). The forum was hosted by UNE, using the program Moodle. It had a URL that included a university-based web address.

Terminology Use in the Study

This study at times used terms in specific ways. The use of the criteria that participants be FtM transgender was broadly conceived—we used the concept as an ***umbrella term*** to cover a range of people who might come under this category. For example, we aimed to include those born intersex (rather than only those who were assigned a strictly female sex at birth as such), those who identified as genderqueer or a trans-man (rather than only those who identified strictly as male as such), those who had not/did not wish to/could not transition legally/socially/medically (rather than only those who had followed a very specific transition journey). We wished to support the diversity of individuals who self-identified within the category, regardless of the limitations and assumptions that have sometimes been placed upon it by psychologists, doctors and researchers in the past.

Within the questionnaire and blog forum, we sometimes used terms denoting body parts interchangeably. For example, we used chest/breasts, and front hole/boy hole/vagina to indicate particular parts, in awareness that different individuals might experience a body part in different ways related to gender identity. This sort of language use was achieved on advice of both the reference group, and later some individual participants. We wished to support the varying framings of bodies accessed by the Australian FtM transgender community, and sought to include both participants who were more, or less, exposed to such terms through supplying alternatives and (at times) definitions when needed.

Ethical Considerations

Ethical approval was obtained for this project from the University of New England Human Research Ethics Committee. An important ethical consideration was the level of freedom and control participants would have in engaging with the study. All participants had the right not to answer any (or all) questions in the survey or forum, the right to withdraw, and the ability to comment on questions or advise the researchers on their wording and so on. The participants also enjoyed opportunities to suggest alternative lines of questioning or topics they felt should be discussed (either in the 'Other' section of the forum, or within the topic areas). Several participants utilised the opportunity to make suggestions about how FtM transgender Australians should/could be constructed in this report and why this would/would not be useful.

As another measure to allow participants extra control over how they were constructed, we afforded all forum bloggers the opportunity to choose their own pseudonym. They could choose words, false names or numbers of their own making, which could be used to express their gender adequately and appropriately, or perhaps to particularly offer ambiguity/extra anonymity (in the case of numbers). However, because some Australian FtM transgender individuals are well known to each other, we included a request for respect for the need for confidentiality on the forum; requesting participants not to harass each-other into revealing their forum names off-line, or their real identities online, on the off-chance they might somehow recognise each-others' stories.

Another key consideration was the protection of all participants from experiencing difficulties in the process of completing the survey and/or the blog, particularly around the mental health questions and the reflections on what could have been difficult life periods. We were careful to be respectful in our wording of questions, and the details of key support services were provided through the survey and forum. In addition, trained psychologists were available to assist people through the moderation of sites by the *E-males* research team. We also protected all participants from abusive posts by moderating each individual post before it was published, and whilst this meant posts did not immediately appear on the blogs, it ensured there were no abusive/transphobic posts.

The younger participants (aged 16–17) were not required to seek parental approval for their participation in the study. This decision was made in recognition of the lack of support—and sometimes discrimination and abuse—that research has shown some young gender questioning people experience in the home. We felt it would be irresponsible to require young people to have to disclose their gender identity in order to participate, and so we ensured the design of the study considered these participants' vulnerability and capacity to give consent, and provided clear information about the research. The young people were separated from the older group (aged 18+) on the blog forum, in recognition of the need to protect younger participants from more adult discussions of key themes such as sexuality, their different experiences/life stages, and also to facilitate separate moderation for the group by experts on youth issues.

Sampling

The target group was Australian FtM transgender people aged 16 and over. Participants needed to self-select to be part of the research. We actively endeavoured to include people from all states and territories of Australia, and from a range of FtM transgender networks and groupings (including those with varying understandings of what FtM identity can comprise).

E-Males Concept and Logo

In celebration of the opportunities to contact FtM transgender Australians through modern technologies, and of the online supports and communities now available, we named this study *E-males*. This name was also used for its interesting play on the words used to denote sex and gender, modern identity and an emphasis on modern males. A logo was also produced in the form of a blue male scientific symbol emerging from a faded female scientific symbol, signifying male identity with a twist, sex/gender transition, affirmation of masculinity and other possible meanings that could be relevant to a diverse range of FtM people. While we knew some participants would identify squarely as men, we felt that the gender history they'd experienced was certainly in focus in the study, and so we needed to indicate this in the logo. This option for the logo (Fig. 2.1) was most widely supported by the reference group and our networks.

Fig. 2.1 The *E-males* logo

Recruitment and Promotion

The survey and forum were opened in April 2013, when active recruitment began. They were closed at the end of July 2013, after a total of fourth months. We used a range of media to promote the project: FtM transgender Groups/Networks/Services, mainstream/GLBTIQ/FtM transgender media (print, electronic and radio), social networking sites, websites, e-lists, emails, gender clinics, rights groups, individual advocates and rights champions, and word-of-mouth.

Press Release/Media

A press release describing the project was designed by marketing staff and sent out to key mainstream and alternative media, including print and radio. The project was featured in several print news stories, special features in magazines and live radio interviews (Fig. 2.2).

Internet, E-Lists, Networking

Some key Australian FtM transgender groups (and related transgender, genderqueer and other GLBTIQ groups) organise their contact online through websites and e-lists. It was therefore important that recruitment processes developed new online

Fig. 2.2 The *E-males* project advertised by LOTL

contacts to increase the potential reach of the survey. The researchers constructed information about the project that could be sent to groups, and then emailed and called people running these groups, sites and lists. This information was widely disseminated throughout the contacts of these groups and networks. For example, FtM Australia was able to contact over 800 people on their list. Transmen Australia, DUDE Magazine, the National LGBTIQ Health Alliance, Ygender and others also gave the project wonderful support.

Social Networking Sites

Due to the popularity of social networking as means for sharing information and facilitating community contact for FtM transgender people, we created a Facebook page and also circulated posts on the project through online pages, sites and groups. The "I'm Transgender Facebook" Page, Trans Health Australia Page, Open Doors Page, Australian Transgender Proud, Trans Panther SA, Transgender Victoria (TGV) Page, GSMA Page and many others featured our posts.

Gender Centres

Gender Centres around Australia displayed leaflets and posters with information about the project, or passed on information to interested community members. We also bought some paid advertisements where available. For example, Fig. 2.3 shows project information featured on the Zoe Belle Gender Centre's website.

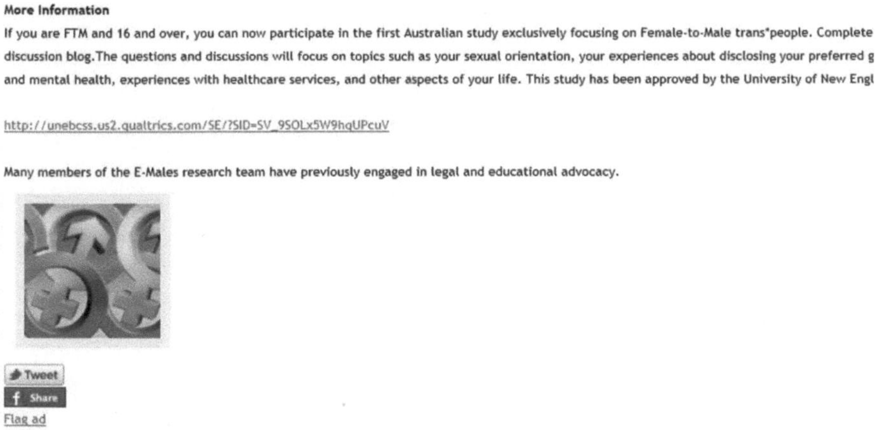

Fig. 2.3 An *E-males* advertisement on the Zoe Belle Gender Centre website

Data Analysis

Data were downloaded from the survey site and then transposed into quantitative (SPSS v10) and qualitative (Leximancer, Excel) computer programs. Descriptive and comparative statistical analyses were undertaken, and thematic analyses of written responses. All significant differences in the report are calculated at 0.05, however, to ensure the accessibility of the report, specific statistical results are not presented here. The journeys of many *E-males* participants are also displayed within this report.

Chapter 3
Our Diverse FtM Transgender Participants

Abstract In total, 273 FtM transgender people participated in the *E-males* project in 2013; the largest number of FtM transgender people in an Australian study. This chapter provides some basic demographic information about these diverse respondents. Participants ranged in age from 16 to 64, with the average age 30.5. The participants came from all states of Australia, but were slightly more concentrated in Victoria and in urban areas than the broader population. They represented a range of culturally and linguistically diverse (CALD) backgrounds. In terms of allocated sex at birth, 97 % of the participants were allocated a female sex at birth, and 3 % were intersex. In terms of gender identity, most participants identify as male, but other identities (such as FtM transgender, transsexual male, genderqueer and so on) were represented. The group mostly lived in stable situations with loved ones, and were mostly working or studying. A large majority had no religious affiliation.

Keywords Transgender · FtM · Transsexual · Male · Genderqueer · Demographics · Age · Research · Data · Study

> The trans* 'culture' that's sprung up in my generation is not one I get along with, and I like to avoid it when possible (junk000, male, 22 years).
>
> I have a roof over my head, food in my belly when I need it, and am studying in a course I'm totally passionate about. It's a good place to be in, considering this time last year I was homeless due to bad family circumstances because of my sexuality (Hansel, genderqueer, 22 years).

Key Findings

- 273 people participated in the *E-males* project.
- Participants ranged in age from 16 to 64, with the average age 30.5.
- All Australian states were represented in the study.
- 97 % of the participants were allocated a female sex at birth, 3 % intersex.

T. Jones et al., *Female-to-Male (FtM) Transgender People's Experiences in Australia*, SpringerBriefs in Sociology, DOI 10.1007/978-3-319-13829-9_3

- 51 % of participants identify as male, but other identities (such as FtM transgender, transsexual male, genderqueer and so on) were also represented.
- The group mostly lived in stable situations with their loved ones.
- 86 % of the group had no religious affiliation.

Number of Participants

While many people responded to this first national survey of Female-to-Male Transgender Australians, those who did not fit the criteria were removed from the study. The criteria included age (16+), location (reside in Australia) and identification as FtM transgender (in its broadest sense—including people who were born intersex, people who are genderqueer and so on). This left us with 273 valid *E-males* participants; the largest group of Female-to-Male Transgender people in an Australian study.

How Participants Came to the Study

Participants mainly came to the study through informal posts and paid advertising featured on webpages (41 %), and a further 27 % came to the study through a friend. In addition, 31 % came to the study through other connections: many of these routes were via FTM Australia e-list invites, contact made through Ozguys, Trangender Victoria, Ygender, Zoe Belle Gender Centre, FTM Shed, Open Doors QLD, Star Observer LOTL Magazine, Tumblr, SSO, DUDE Magazine and other media, support services and social groups who supported the study in various ways. There were also people who heard interviews about the project on Joy FM or other radio stations, saw it discussed through their Facebook group (such as the group QT for T Boys) or were referred to it by someone at a gender centre (Fig. 3.1).

Age

The *E-males* participants represented a diverse range of age groups. The youngest were 16, the oldest were 64. The majority of participants were aged in their 20s and 30s, the average age was 30.5. This is younger than in *Tranznation* for example, but older than the group of transgender and gender questioning students in *Writing Themselves in 3* (Fig. 3.2).

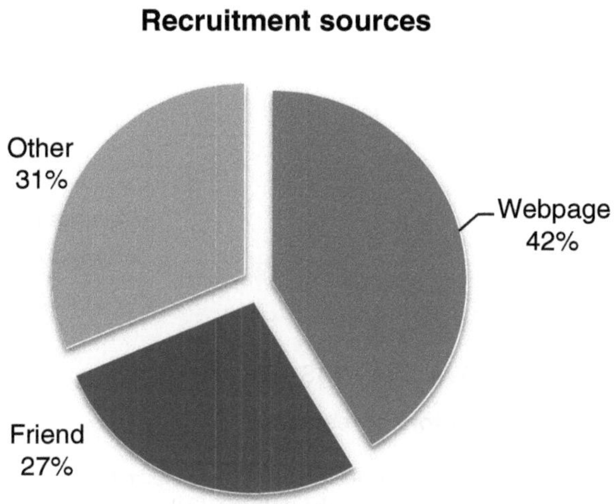

Fig. 3.1 *E-males study* recruitment sources for participants (n = 226)

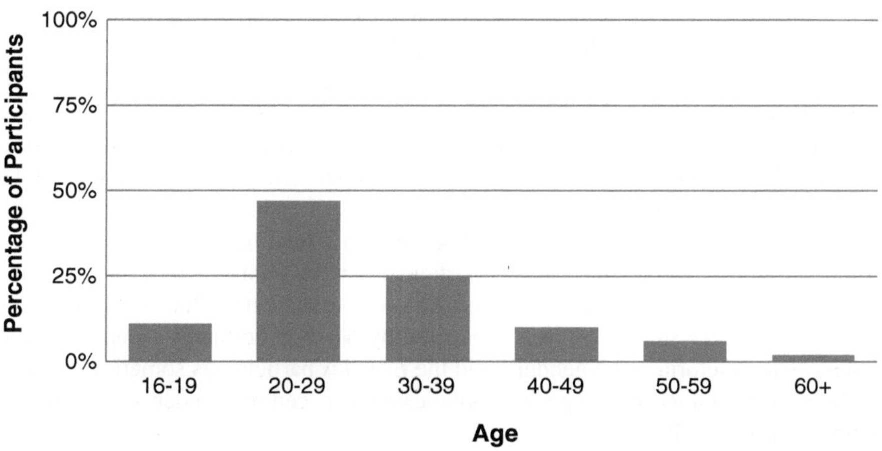

Fig. 3.2 Age of *E-males* participants (n = 256)

State/Territory

The location of the participants' place of residence was determined through an analysis of the postcodes they provided. The range of postcodes revealed the participants came from every state in Australia, which was an achievement. Efforts were made to recruit respondents in proportion to the general population of each Australian state and territory. However, most participants came from Victoria (39 %) and New South Wales (30 %). There were also participants from Queensland (15 %) and Western Australia (9 %), with lower numbers coming from

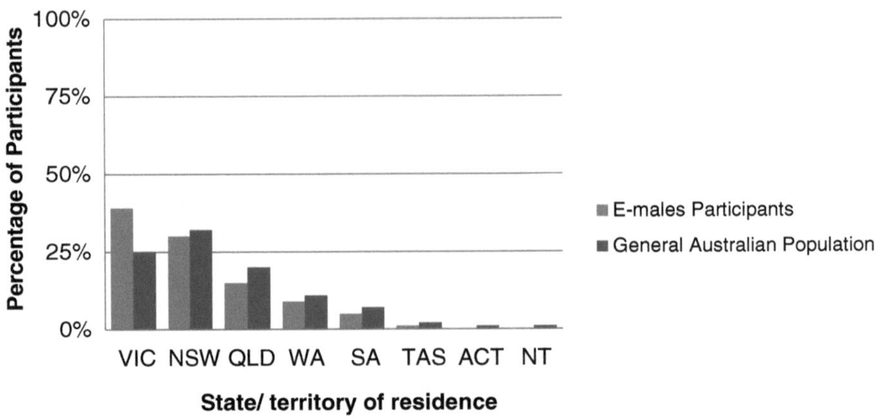

Fig. 3.3 Residence of *E-males* participants (n = 99) compared to the general Australian population (n = 22,906,400) [As reported by the ABS (2012)]

SA (5 %) and Tasmania (1 %). Less than 1 % of the group came from each of the territories (the Australian Capital Territory and Northern Territory), and we note that a few participants discussed moving from these locations in order to access specific services in places like Melbourne and Sydney.

This population was disproportionately concentrated in urban settings in VIC rather than in other states, and rather than in the rural and remote areas represented, compared to the broader Australian population (Australian Bureau of Statistics 2012c). This contrasts with, for example, the younger same sex attracted and gender questioning population in *Writing Themselves in 3*, who were distributed in a pattern roughly reflective of the general population. The difference is likely due to a combination of factors—the *E-males* participants were on average in their 30s and thus not confined to their families' original homes to the extent that younger people were, the *E-males* study was well-supported by Melbourne-based groups (such as Transgender Victoria and Ygender), and the *E-males* participants sometimes sought to live in locations with specific policies/gender centres/gender experts/social supports in place (Fig. 3.3).

Birth Sex

The majority of the respondents were allocated a female sex at birth (97 %). However, 3 % were defined intersex at birth. Whilst some readers may be surprised at what initially seems like a high portion of respondents who were considered intersex at birth, we note that this figure fits squarely within estimates of the portion of people who are considered intersex within the broader population, suggested by researchers such as Anne Fausto-Sterling and John Money as comprising somewhere between 2 and 4 % (Carroll 2005; Fausto-Sterling 1993; OII Australia 2012).

We also note that it is unfortunately rare for researchers to ask participants in any given study whether they are intersex, or were considered intersex at birth, so data on this matter may seem more unexpected than it really ought to be. Therefore, this study does not particularly suggest that intersex people are more likely to have an FtM transgender (or other transgender) identity than broader populations. However, it does importantly show that both babies allocated a female sex, and those considered intersex, may later identify within the FtM transgender umbrella.

Gender Identity

The participants were asked which gender role/gender identity they identified with. Slightly more than half of the group identified as male (51 %). However, there was also a broad range of identification and self-definition: a further 20 % identified as FtM transgender, 15 % as Genderqueer, 7 % as Transsexual male, and 2 % as female (but still in some sense on the FTM spectrum—whether they were beginning a transition journey, gender questioning or gender non-conforming to a strong extent). A further 4 % gave other terms, including for example transman, male with a twist, boi, myself and so on. Those who identified as male were less likely to think about themselves as "trans" in most environments (but more likely to think of themselves as trans when participating in trans or LGBTIQ contexts/events/support services). They usually defined their FTM experience in relation to having *a trans history*, rather than *being* trans as such. These identities are explored in Chap. 4 (Fig. 3.4).

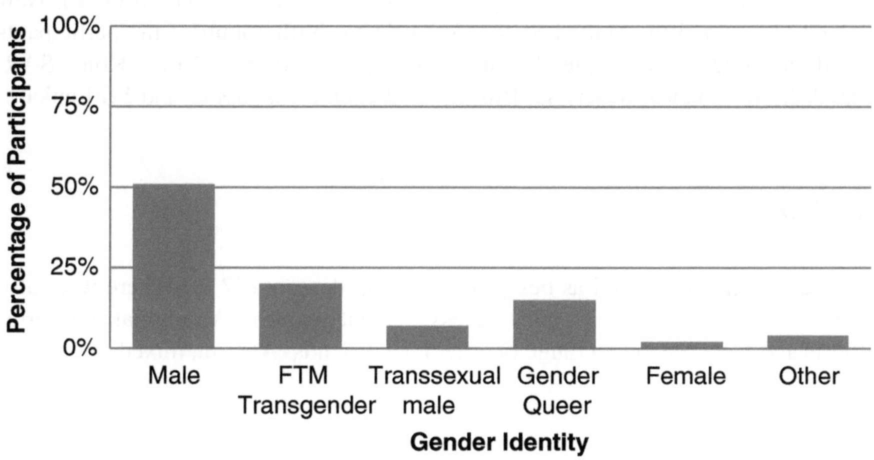

Fig. 3.4 Gender identity of *E-males* participants (n = 229)

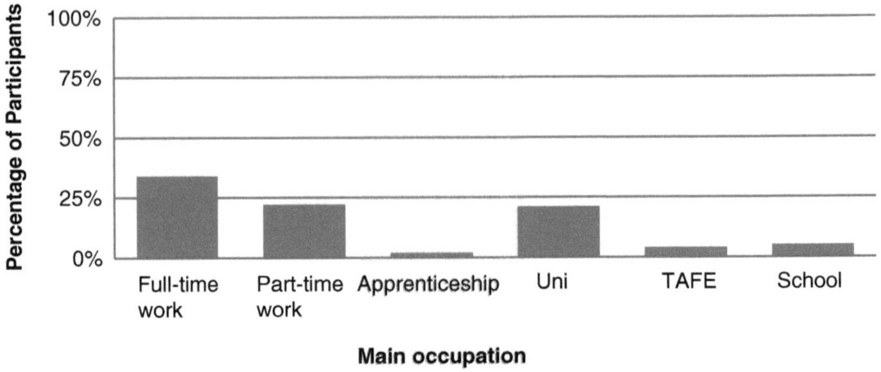

Fig. 3.5 Main occupation of *E-males* participants (n = 237)

Main Occupation

Most *E-males* participants were employed (58 %): full-time (34 %), part-time (22 %), or in an apprenticeship (2 %). The second largest group were engaged in study (30 %): at university (21 %), at school (5 %), or at TAFE (4 %). The remainder were unemployed (15 %) (Fig. 3.5).

Birth Country

The majority (82 %) of *E-males* respondents were born in Australia, and there were portions of the group who were originally from the United Kingdom (4 %), New Zealand (3 %), and the United States (3 %). Other birth countries the participants named included for example Argentina, Canada, Germany, Hong Kong SAR, Ireland, Italy, Jamaica, Malaysia, Russian Federation, Singapore and Sri Lanka.

Ethnicity

Most participants identified as being of European descent (77 %). There were also people of Asian descent (5 %), and to a lesser extent people of Aboriginal and Torres Strait Islander descent and a range of other backgrounds (African, mixed and so on).

Disability

The large majority of participants did not identify as having a disability—an important point to emphasise given the fact that transgender people have historically been construed by some psychological and psychiatric bodies as disordered on the basis of their gender identity alone, and have had to use disability/disorder framings to access services. In total, 17 % of the group identified themselves as having one or more disabilities. In the main these disabilities related to mental health (such as anxiety, bipolar, borderline personality disorder, depression, PTSD and schizophrenia). However there were also individuals with cognitive and social disabilities and learning/processing disorders (such as ADHD, Asperger's, Autism, dyslexia, social phobia and others), and people with physical issues (asthma, chronic fatigue syndrome, chronic pain, Ehlers-Danlos syndrome, epilepsy, hearing impairments, lupus, muscle function and mobility issues, scoliosis, spinal deterioration, synovitis, xxy). More rarely, individuals framed their gender dysphoria as a birth defect and therefore a disability. The overall resistance of FTM Australians to doing so perhaps explains the tensions around classifications of gender identity diagnoses as disorders or otherwise, discussed in the international literature (Drescher 2013).

Living Arrangements

The participants were mostly living in relatively stable situations with their loved ones: 36 % were living with their partner, 26 % with their family, and 14 % with friends. Around 14 % were living alone. A further 8 % described other living arrangements, including living at a military base, house-sharing with acquaintances, living with foster children, minding grandchildren, or living between states for example. Around 2 % reported that they were in more precarious contexts or homeless, couch surfing or living at college temporarily. We believe this might be an under-representation of the incidence of homelessness amongst this group given anecdotal reports, and the high portion of homeless gender questioning youth in *Writing Themselves in 3* (Hillier et al. 2010) (Fig. 3.6).

Religion

In terms of religion, 86 % of the respondents reported that they did not have an affiliation to a religious denomination. This is a strikingly high portion in comparison to the 22 % of Australians with no religious affiliation more broadly (Australian Bureau of Statistics 2012b). There is clearly a message in this statistic—that the mainstream Christian faiths usually so common in Australian society are

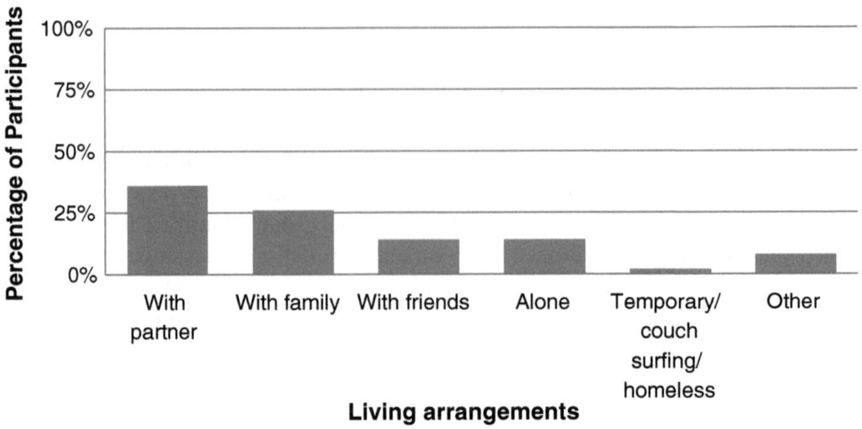

Fig. 3.6 Living arrangements of *E-males* participants (n = 224)

less embraced by, and likely less embracing of, our FtM transgender community. Amongst the 14 % of participants who did have a religious affiliation, the most common denominations were Christian (50 %), Judaism (13 %), Hinduism (3 %), Buddhism (3 %) and Other beliefs (31 %). Of the beliefs nominated by the latter group, the most common was Pagan (including such variations as Neo-Pagan, Pagan Druidry, and Polytheistic Pagan for example). There were also Heathen (Germanic Asatru) and Sikh participants for example.

Chapter 4
Gender Identity

Abstract This chapter explores data on gender identity generated by the 273 FtM transgender Australians in the 2013 *E-Males* study. Most participants (51 %) identified simply as "male". This group tended to have known their identity from a young age, and had struggled with the development of secondary sex characteristics during puberty. However, some were unsure about their identity until later in life. Participants who mainly identified as either "transgender", "trans male", "FTM" or "male with transgender or transsexual background" explained that referring to themselves only as only as male would be to deny part of themselves. "Genderqueer" was the preferred way to self-identify for those who rejected pressures to fit into female-male binary model or stereotypes—whether they did not relate to or agree with the binary, or were uncertain about gender. All participants expressed strong negative feelings against being referred to by female pronouns, regardless of their diverse gender identities.

Keywords Transgender · FtM · Transsexual · Male · Genderqueer · Transman · Boi · Gender · Identity · Pronouns

> Well, I would prefer to identify myself as male, but since I don't pass all that often I sometimes have to tell people I'm a transman. (…) I can't remember not thinking I was male, and I've always known I wasn't physically male, my parents constantly reminded me. I think it really hit hard during high school, because at that time my group of friends stopped seeing me as 'one of the guys' and started seeing me as female. It was depressing. I withdrew from everyone around me and spent lunch times alone. I would read books and play video games and hide in my world of fantasy, because I could be anything I wanted there (Draconem, FtM transgender, 24 years).

> I identify as genderqueer, in the sense of feeling neither female nor male. Personally I find the social construction of binary gender identities as oppressive and distorting. I don't believe that human attitudes, abilities, personality traits, and behaviours can or should be divided into two discrete categories and allocated to particular sexed bodies. Knowing that I was born with XX genotype and female reproductive organs tells you absolutely nothing about me that is important or even relevant (except insofar as I've had to struggle against that and all society's investments in that to come into my personhood) (Shourya, genderqueer, 55 years).

T. Jones et al., *Female-to-Male (FtM) Transgender People's Experiences in Australia*, SpringerBriefs in Sociology, DOI 10.1007/978-3-319-13829-9_4

Key Findings

- Most *E-males* participants (51 %) identify simply as "male". Some of these men occasionally referred to themselves as "genderqueer" or "transgender" when in a GLBTIQ context.
- Participants who mainly identified as either "transgender", "trans male", "FTM" or "male with transgender or transsexual background" explained that referring to themselves only as only as male would deny a part of themselves.
- "Genderqueer" was the preferred way to self-identify for those who rejected pressures to fit into female-male binary model or stereotypes—either since they did not relate to or agree with the binary, or due to an uncertainty about gender.
- Despite their diversity, all participants expressed strong negative feelings about being referred to by female pronouns.
- Most of the participants had an awareness of gender incongruence from a very early age, and displayed behaviours traditionally associated with boys.

Self-Identification

In the survey the participants were asked which gender role they identified with. Slightly more than half of the group (51 %) identified as male. A further 20 % identified as FtM transgender, 15 % as Genderqueer, 7 % as Transgender Male and 2 % as Female but within the FTM spectrum (given their stage of transitioning). There was no correlation between age and identity, which the researchers found surprising, as we expected that perhaps there would be certain "conceptualisations of self" more common to younger or older groups. However, people of varying ages identified as either male or genderqueer for example. It seemed that perhaps the internet and other cultural hubs have made different conceptualisations of gender identity equally available to younger and older groups (from which they could then navigate a path to their own understandings of self), and that age alone does not explain identity constructions (Fig. 4.1).

Selection of Pseudonyms

The *E-males* participants were encouraged to select their own pseudonyms for the study. This was important so that their gender was appropriately captured, and so that they had some control over how they were constructed in any publications from the research. These names were also used by the participants to interact with others, and talk about themselves on the *E-males* forum. The pseudonyms the respondents selected revealed elements of their gender identity in interesting ways, and could be grouped together in categories according to the types of identity messages they

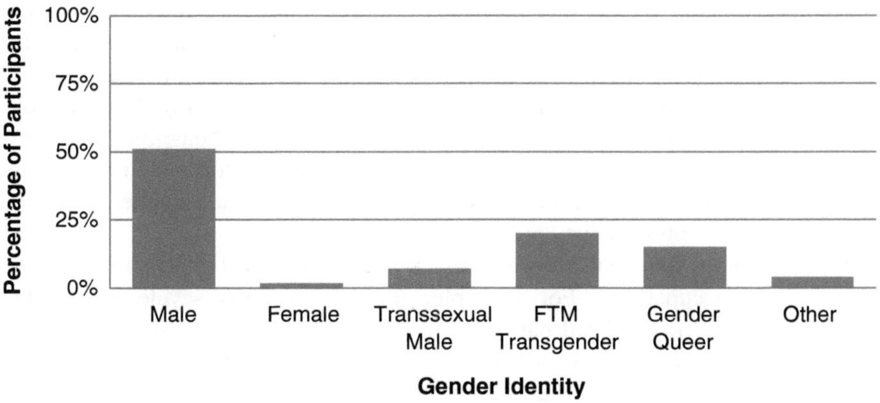

Fig. 4.1 Gender identity of the *E-males* participants (n = 229)

conveyed. Whilst there was the opportunity to simply use a random number, most of the group seemed to enjoy developing a name of a more revealing character.

The most common type of pseudonym selected was a mainstream male name, including such examples as "John", "Mike", and "Peter" (which are all very common names across the Australian male population generally). In many ways this was unsurprising given that the largest group of participants saw themselves simply as male, and presented themselves as such (rather than focussing on their transgender/transsexual past) in most social contexts. It made sense that even on a forum for FtM transgender people, this group of men would continue to classify themselves as fairly generic male types. Also common was the use of indicators of male identity that were not "names" as such, but were male referents, pronouns or honorifics generally used to address or discuss males. For example, "Mister", "Mr Dude", or names including "boy" or "man" within them as a prefix or suffix. There was no particular discernible pattern of correlation between age and pseudonym, with both younger and older participants using male names to the same degree (such as alex342 who was 16 years, and Toby who was 62 years) and using boy or man interchangeably.

Another group of pseudonyms focussed more visibly on transgender-related identities, which played on related to terms such as FtM, transman, GID and so on. For example, there were participants who used "sstrans", "GladlyGiddy" or "ftm-boy" as their name for the study. Related to this theme, some respondents incorporated actions or activities related to being an FtM transgender person or to transitioning in their name. For example, "PackinTman" incorporated the concept of "packing" (wearing padding or a phallic object in one's pants or underwear) and taking "t" (testosterone), highlighting how these behaviours were intimately related to his construction of self. This group overall was smaller than the first, which fit the finding that identifying as FtM transgender or Transsexual male was less common. There were also names indicating genderqueer status or gender disruption such as "girlboywonder", somewhat reflecting the occurence of genderqueer identity.

Another popular theme was the use of animals and animal-related terms in pseudonyms. The animals were almost exclusively large, fierce and powerful. The animals selected also tended to be of the type where males of the breed largely lived alone, which perhaps added to a sense of their masculine autonomy. Key examples were "dragon", "draconem" (a latin variation on dragon), and "daggboy" (a type of large old African buffalo bull found in Zimbabwe, that is notoriously grumpy, and has generally been kicked out of its herd). There were also some smaller, less fierce animal-name exceptions (like "pig" and "prawn").

Some of the respondents chose to use indicators of involvement in masculine activities or occupations. For example, there were motor-cycle names like "Harleyguy", and tool-related names such as "chainsaw". There were other occupation-related names such as "the doctor", "grumpylumberjack", "photoman" and similar. There were also other relatively masculine identities like "punk13", "lostprince" and "viking". Related to this group of pseudonyms was the use of famous male writers' names like "Byron", "Dante", "Kafka" and others.

There were other smaller themes. For example, there were pseudonyms designed to enhance or engage with anonymity such as "shadow", "falsename", "qwerty", "Q", "cj", "J223" and number combinations. There were pseudonyms incorporating indicators of possible sexual identities and interests such as "zbdsm" (which included within it the acronym bdsm—representing bondage, discipline, and sadomasochism) and similar. The several "bear" identities ("bear", "excited bear", "cubby" and others) which appeared related to GLBTIQ community notions of large, relatively hirsute gay and bisexual men (and increasingly transgender men) and related masculine subcultures. The participants did not declare that they were members of such subcultures however—these choices might simply have been because the terms were common as GLBTIQ discussion board names. Lastly, there were pseudonyms related to community activism, such as "solidarity", "gentlemenunite" and "Boycott".

Defining and Describing Gender Identity

The male participants mainly stated that they felt they were not different to other "cis(gender) males", or that they were "just like any other bloke". This category of participants made frequent reference in the blog to an incongruence between their mind and body, with statements like "*I was born with a female body and a male mind*" (Brett, male/transgender male, 27 years); "*I define my gender by my psychology*" (Gavin, male/FtM transgender, 23 years); and "*(male) is the sex of my brain*" (Nikozilar, male, 20 years). In one example, a man explained an increasingly common line of thinking in and beyond the transgender community:

> Gender identity is your innate sense of gender whether it be male, female or other. It has nothing to do with your biological sex (thewaywesee, trans* male or queer male, 22 years).

Similarly, Jay commented further on this separation of gender and body:

> My gender identity is now and has always been male. Although having been socialised as "female" during my upbringing, I wouldn't classify myself as a complete blokey bloke, I'm a little more sensitive than your average Joe but there isn't much that's feminine about me either. Even seeing the parts of my body that are not that typical of a natal born male, I still see myself as male because I don't see these parts as belonging to me (Jay, male, 30 years).

Others expressed the desire to identify themselves as male, but explained that they were not yet comfortable enough to use that term given the stage of transitioning they were at. These respondents felt their gender was evolving, but that based on their physical characteristics, they felt "caught in the middle of two genders". It would appear that participants in these situations did not feel fully *entitled* to identify with their gender of choice (male) until their bodies could reflect this identity without ambiguity or (as some felt) apparent contradiction. For many being "transgender" was considered only as a stage in the process of becoming fully realised as "male":

> Sometimes, in a queer community setting, I might disclose that I'm a person of trans* history, where it's relevant to discussion, but I see that as part of my personal history rather than my gender identity (garfield, male, 31 years).

This concern about being "man enough" to assert a male identity reflected other international studies on FtM people (Yerke and Mitchell 2011).

Some participants who identified as "transgender", "transsexual" or "FTM" in public situations, expressed that they could not deny their experiences or upbringing as a female. Others chose these terms because they felt they were a complex "mix" of gender and sex expressions, rather than strictly one sex or the other. Maddox explained, "*I believe that I fit into the gender of ftm/transman more so than male because although my brain-sex is defiantly male I have been raised as female*" (Maddox, male/ftm/transman, 21 years). Additionally, some of this group indicated that defining themselves in public with transgender labels was a useful way to demystify transgender issues, and empower other people in similar situations. Several explained that when it was necessary to identify themselves as a transgender man to share their story they did so, in order to help others understand what it meant to be transgender or to help somebody deal with their own gender questioning. This was an affirming perspective that suggested that an increasing sense of pride has developed within transgender communities over time, which could go a way towards impacting issues of visibility.

Within those participants who identified as "Genderqueer", some expressed the desire to embody mainly masculine physical attributes. For example, Hansel (genderqueer, age 22 years) reflected, "*I take hormones so that my physical body can match the way I feel but I don't have to pick a side. I am me*". Other genderqueer participants liked to look "visually ambiguous", or expressed a strong stand against societal binary conventions:

> I identify as genderqueer in the sense of feeling neither female nor male. Personally, I find the social constructions of binary gender identities as oppressive and distorting. I don't believe that human attitudes, abilities, personality traits and behaviour can or should be divided in two discrete categories and allocated to particular sexed bodies (Shourya, genderqueer, 55 years).

Despite their personal preferences, participants mentioned other factors that influenced the way they identified. These included relevance to an interpersonal exchange or social context, their level of closeness with others in a given scenario, safety concerns, and their ability to "pass" (as male or even as transgender). For Aid, a sense of fluctuating gender identity, dependent on external and internal factors, was described:

> My gender identity is defined largely at the moment by how society views me, but it is also defined by how I view myself. It's like my view of myself is affected and changed by how I am treated by others (Aid, socially male, 18 years).

Mark 2 (FtM transgender, 57 years) was also influenced by social context, saying "it is hard for me to describe my version of identity, because I am only out to some people, but not to some significant others". He felt male, but had to act female at times. "*Strangers tend to see me as male, but there are also these embarrassing situations when they do a double take*", he said. He found binary gender definitions far too restrictive, and disliked male and female stereotyping. He said that for a long time "*I thought I was some unique freak*", so that having at least some information and some opportunity to express male aspects of himself in some social contexts was "*already a major improvement*".

Age of Discovery

We explored how the participants came to discover their FtM transgender identities. Three broad developmental trajectories emerged in the participants' first awareness of gender incongruence:

- An early and ongoing awareness;
- A series of fluctuating periods of awareness; or
- A lack of awareness accompanied by an inexplicably strong sense of discomfort until late adolescence/early adulthood.

Most participants fell in the first category and expressed that they had an early, clear and ongoing awareness of gender-body incongruence. This group generally had a male identity, and as children had a strong sense of wrong embodiment (they thought of themselves as a "boy") for as long as they could remember. As children this manifested in refusals to wear girls' clothes; having a preference to play with boys and boys' toys; participating in contact sports; playing masculine roles and adopting male physical postures (including for many, trying to urinate as a boy). In addition, they felt a strong desire to develop or replicate male genitalia. They would have dreams about growing a penis or have the conviction that one day they would wake up as a male. For example, *Lance* (male/transsexual male, 40 years) recalled that at four years old he would start each morning by checking to see if he was a boy. He was "really upset" afterwards as he started each day with the discovery that he was not. Sometimes the men reported looking to external or supernatural interventions even as children; with comments such as "*I was 3 or 4 when I asked Santa to bring a sex change*"; or "*I used to pray to God that my breasts would never grow*". *photoman* (male, 41 years) knew his identity from four years old, and remembered resisting all efforts to make him wear dresses or do what he considered to be feminine activities. He recalled getting a doll as a birthday present from his parents and proceeding to rip it to pieces right in front of them. *Zane* (male, 41 years), said "*I was aware from a very early age, although it didn't distress me greatly until I hit puberty. It was easier to fantasise as a child that I would naturally grow up to be male*". *Their early feelings of difference,* magical thinking and daydreaming, and early attempts at "making the change" reflected the themes in the international research (Pazos 2000).

For these participants the emergence of female secondary sexual characteristics during puberty was quite traumatic. It brought a strong sense of disgust, embarrassment, withdrawal, isolation and consequent depression. Nikozilar recalled:

> When I was really little, I thought I was a boy. I didn't realize that I wasn't. I was really weirded out by my genitalia and I deliberately hurt it. The day I got my period, depression hit like a brick. Suddenly I knew there was something seriously wrong (Nikozilar, male, 20 years).

In our clinical and educational support work with young FtM transgender Australians, the authors have similarly come across young people who had harmed their bodies during puberty, including one boy who—in seeking to burn his breasts off—had set his entire body alight. He had suffered terrible burns and life-long injury to his limbs and skin. Whilst this was an extreme case, there is a sense amongst clinicians and support services that puberty can come as more of a shock to FtM transgender youth (due to the decreasing lack of acceptance of "tomboys" in the teen years, and the onset of menstruation and breast development), than to some MtF Transgender youth—who tend to have already experienced great difficulties in earlier years due to the lack of acceptance in Australian culture of (so-called) boys (who feel they are girls) wearing long hair or dresses.

Suddenly being unable to go topless in public, trying to dress a curvier body that used to fit well into boys' clothes but no longer complied, being made unwelcome in male groups (at skate parks, sports or elsewhere) were all described as confronting and distressful moments that often led to long periods of depression. Xzaclee (male, 35 years) described how as a child he "*was aware that I didn't have the same gentials as my mates*", but at a young age that "*didn't bother me*". However, it was only as he grew older that he understood the difference and its impact, and "*fantasised about having a penis*". *JW (*Male/ftm/slightly Genderqueer, 19 years) similarly wanted to grow a penis, and had tensions with his mother over trying to get other people to agree that he was male. Harleyguy (transsexual male,

40 years) resented the sudden expectation of feminine behaviour that arose around puberty, particularly when he was in public. Whilst some people went to extreme measures to deal with these issues, others withdrew into a world of books, reading or video games to avoid social engagement, distract or comfort themselves. This reflected international clinicians' accounts of the traumatic nature of puberty for their transsexual clients generally, and specifically FtM people, and the trend to dissociation as a coping mechanism (Brown and Rownsley 1996; Pazos 2000).

However, a second and different trajectory was followed by some participants, who during their childhood and teenage years experienced fluctuating periods of awareness that they did not satisfy or fit the traditional gender expectations. This group actively suppressed this awareness as a "truth too painful to endure", because they thought there was no solution. Sometimes this effort to ignore thoughts and feelings about their gender was related to their parents' negative reactions (dismissal or rejection) upon the disclosure of their gender identities:

> I had moments as a teen where I knew. But I suppressed it all. It all came crashing down around me when I was about 20. It happened when I saw the results of one guy's transition. I guess I didn't know that transitioning was possible until then. I think that's why I suppressed it, because I didn't know there was an answer (Harry, FtM transgender, 24 years).

Sam (male/transguy, 22 years) said "*I spent a little while trying to deny/ignore it, but also did a lot of research into transitioning at the same time*". GladlyGiddy (male, 55 years) had always considered himself as a boy as far back as he could remember, but had to repress this due to his family's responses. At age two he tried to pee like a boy but always wet his pants trying. His mother thought he was regressing in his toilet training. He was rejected by the boys he wanted to play with in his teens and realised he would not be one of them, and was pressured by family and friends to "become a lady". He was often called a lesbian or a butch, and had many straight women become attracted to him, but ignored these taunts and tried to integrate into life as a woman. He got married to try to fit in. He was only ready to face his GID at 45. At 55 he is now "*taking the bullet by the teeth and going ahead with being a hairy, deep voiced, large breasted male until the 2 years are up and I am able to go through chest surgery*".

The remaining participants followed a third trajectory; they described a sense of inexplicable discomfort and dysphoria throughout childhood and adolescence, but claimed that a clearer understanding and awareness of "why" they felt this way only came later in life. They reported always feeling different, "ugly", "ill-fitting", and depressed; but not knowing that this discomfort was actually about their gender. Alex (transgender man/transman/transguy, 48 years) similarly felt different from age 10 but had no idea why "*until I left home in my twenties and investigated further*". He felt leaving home allowed him the freedom to consider his life's direction more decisively. Ramir (transgender, 25 years) felt "*different my whole life*," without a strong sense of why. Anthony (male, FtM transgender, 19 years) experienced additional complications coming from a culture "*which is very separatist when it come to gender*", so he mainly had to be around girls and felt like "*an alien around others*". The confusion often brought people to sexual experimentation, to find out who they were during late adolescence or young adulthood. Many participants had lesbian relationships and identified as such for a time, but continued experiencing dysphoria until they had the realization they were transgender. This generally occurred as a result of having access to relevant information on gender diversity or meeting a transgender person. On many occasions this newly acquired self-knowledge brought a deep sense of relief, depression vanished or significantly improved and the individuals then started the gradual journey of transitioning. Ramir reflected that, "*looking back, knowing that I was transgender makes my whole life make sense*". Doc79 had a similar life-changing realisation:

> When puberty hit, I sank into deep depression, knowing something was wrong, but not knowing what it was. I was interested in girls but I knew I wasn't gay. Then at university I met a teacher who was trans* and this changed my life (doc79, male, 33 years).

For the genderqueer participants, moments of discovery had more to do with exposure to queer and post-modernist feminist theory. They also mentioned particular books covering gender concepts, or periods of their life where they engaged in formal study that helped inform their perspectives on their different experiences of gender to cisgendered people.

Gender Identity Clinics

We wanted to investigate the value of gender clinics and related services in assisting in understanding one's gender identity. There was however a strong message from the data that there was a distinct lack of gender identity clinics in Australia, or related experts and services, by comparison to need. Many participants had never had access to gender clinics through which to discuss or understand gender identity issues. These participants often reported a lack of readily available information at the beginning of their transition journey. For instance, Conor (male, queer, trans*, person of colour, 24 years) said he had no engagement whatsoever with services of any kind. Darkneko (FtM transgender, 21 years) said "*There are no gender identity clinics operating in my area. The sexual health clinic only deals with GLB issues*"; Eric (FtM transgender, age 49 years) said he had no access to relevant counsellors and had hoped to use the study to get information, and Junk000 (male, 22 years) even asked the researchers "*What is a gender identity clinic? I got my information through a queer youth group which included gender questioning support*". A group of participants had moved to Victoria and New South Wales in order to access services not available elsewhere. Several participants talked about clinics closing down—particularly in Brisbane, Queensland.

Others talked about how there were different policies in the different Australian states and territories that impacted their access to prescriptions for hormonal treatment, clinic services and the need to travel long distances from rural areas to see a prescribing psychiatrist. Garfield explained some of the problems that arise when different contexts have different requirements:

> When I first started investigating transition, the state I was living in did have a gender identity service, but there was a 6-12 month waiting list to be seen. I didn't really want to wait that long, I wanted to be transitioned socially before I finished uni so that I didn't have problems in my professional career. So I found a friendly GP and got the names of a friendly psychiatrist and friendly endo from friends who WERE going through the gender clinic, and asked to be referred. That worked OK for me. Then, I moved interstate and managed to find a local GP who would keep my prescription up without needing to go through the gender clinic, based on letters from my former psychiatrist and endo. Then I moved states again and HAD to go through the gender clinic, because it was the law there. That was really awful because I lived in a rural area and it was a 4 h round trip into see the gender clinic psychiatrist every 6 weeks (expensive and I had to keep taking days off work) until I met the criteria in that state (different from where I started transitioning) for my GP to manage my testosterone prescription without oversight. It would be great if the laws were nationally consistent, and a bit less restrictive – especially for people in rural areas who might not have easy access to services.

There was a strong sense that unless one lived in the right area (particularly inner-city Melbourne or Sydney), one's access to gender identity clinics would be problematic.

Fang (FtM transgender, 29 years), like many others, found that going to regular GPs to discuss gender identity issues (as opposed to centres, clinics and services specifically designed for transgender people), also presented difficulties. He went to four doctors before finding one who would listen to him, and one had even asked, "*why would you want to change your gender, you're such a pretty girl?*" Fang reflected that disclosing something so personal to a stranger "*is a HUGE deal,*" and that to "*be brushed off like that is just fucking bullshit*". He also described how a GP who referred him to a psychiatrist for assessment and now prescribes his hormone injections "*wrote me a medical certificate last week and plastered "SHE" all over it!*" The doctor's use of female pronouns "devastated" him, and he was unable to get it amended before having to give it to staff at his educational institution, whom he was seeking to educate about his gender identity—"*It was a big blow and really undermining*". It took over a year from the first referral to the first psychiatric appointment; the process was "*drawn out, disempowering, expensive and anxiety triggering*". Each step of the way Fang felt he met yet another person "*who won't believe me*". He felt that rather being given the information and assistance he needed, he had to try to predict what he was "supposed" to say each session, and he would often have anxiety about "*if I had said the 'right' thing to pass, or 'will I pass?' like my gender identity is a test*" because traditional binary sex notions informed the doctors' overly stereotypical view of how a male should act/think.

Many other participants referred to the lack of training doctors and even some experts appeared to have around transgender issues. They described having to endure anxiety-provoking processes to "qualify" for transition or other treatment. They also discussed the difficulty, given this dearth of professionals, in checking their credentials or prior work in the field as one might normally wish to for a potential medical professional/surgeon in a specialist area. Conversely, Doc79 found that one NSW-based doctor was "great" in his management of hormones and life issues when he first was questioning his gender. He found a clinic in another state was very supportive too and "after one meeting with its head they ok'd me for lower surgery", which he proceeded to have. Whilst he was glad it was "hassle free", Doc79 felt there should be "some more restraints before changing peoples' bodies" in ways that can't be reversed; "you can't get a person's true identity from one visit… you need multiple visits to establish a pattern of identity". He felt that he personally had a smooth transition but recommended that more measures needed to be put in place to check on the wellbeing of patients and the appropriateness and progression of treatments. The contrast between individuals' experiences of time before approval for transition, investigation into their gender identity, supportiveness of service-providers and levels of expertise were incredibly concerning. It revealed a lack of consistent training, a lack of auditing and lack of research-based standards of care. The next chapter takes a deeper look at concepts and experiences of transitioning.

Chapter 5
Transitioning and Other Options

Abstract Transgender people may engage in transition (or self-affirmation) processes with any or all of personal, internal, social, legal and physical elements. This chapter discusses data on transitioning generated by the 273 FtM transgender Australians in the 2013 *E-Males* study. In terms of physical transitions, non-surgical measures were the most common, and a strong majority of participants had used binding and hormones (87 %). Most (73 %) have had physical interventions to make their body look more masculine and 70 % intend to have additional modifications—chest surgeries were the most popular type. Almost half of the participants spent between $1,000 and $10,000 in this process. The great majority (97 %) expressed that these interventions have made a difference to their life and well-being, even when results were not optimal. Most participants were satisfied or very satisfied with their interventions. Some participants reported difficulties in their efforts to change their names and sex on documentation.

Keywords Transgender · Transition · Change · Surgery · Hormones · Bind · Chest · Genital · Cost · Satisfaction

> I started out with binders and packers, have been on hormones since 2009. In the past year I have now had chest surgery and a full hysterectomy. All up, I reckon I would have spent at least $15k. Chest surgery alone was $10k. My injections until this year were $140 every 12 weeks. Binders were about $30-40 each and I had like 6 of them. Packers are anywhere from $15-50 each depending on if they're STP enabled or not. My hysterectomy was of no cost to me on the public health system. I'm very satisfied with the results. I do however require a revision on my chest. It has all made a massive difference to my life. I feel more at home in my own skin that I ever have. I have more confidence and I am more outgoing and generally more into living my life rather than just existing as I was prior to transitioning. I intend to have further genital reconstruction surgery in the form of a phalloplasty in the next year or so. Although I know a penis doesn't make someone a man or not, for me it is something I have always wanted and felt I was missing and I plan to rectify that to enable me to feel whole and complete. I am currently liaising with surgeons overseas for my phalloplasty, purely because it is not available in Australia at all (Jay, male, 30 years).

> I'm not interested in bottom surgery right now, and don't experience a huge amount of dysphoria regarding my genitals. I enjoy sex a lot, and have no desire to change how I have it (Conor, male, queer, trans*, person of colour, 24 years).

T. Jones et al., *Female-to-Male (FtM) Transgender People's Experiences in Australia*, SpringerBriefs in Sociology, DOI 10.1007/978-3-319-13829-9_5

Key Findings

- Most of the *E-male* participants (73 %) have had physical interventions to make their body look more masculine and 70 % intend to have additional modifications.
- Almost half of the participants spent between $1,000 and $10,000 in this process.
- The great majority (97 %) expressed that these interventions have made a difference to their life and the way the feel, even when surgical results were not optimal.
- 79 % stated that their level of satisfaction with the results of the interventions ranged between somewhat satisfied and very satisfied.
- In a 10 point scale where participants were required to rate their current physical appearance from feminine (0) to masculine (10), the average number rated at a 7.
- No participant reported having to break the law, engage in the black market, use unapproved treatments or someone else's prescriptions to transition. For those who had been tempted, safety concerns had prevented them from doing so.

Diverse Forms of Transitioning

Most of the *E-males* participants had engaged in one or more forms of intervention to express their gender, although it is important to clarify that not all participants saw these interventions as part of a transition path. For many transitioning was a process involving various acts and interventions on the path to realising or affirming male identity. But for a smaller group the modifications were an expression of a genderqueer or alternate identity, or part of a "natural transition" into being more themselves as individuals rather than into becoming male as such. Transitioning could have any or all of personal/internal, social, legal and physical elements. In terms of physical transitions, non-surgical measures were the most common, which made sense in light of their lower cost, accessibility and relevance to a range of conceptions of identity or transition/self-affirmation. A strong majority had used binding and hormones (87 %). In addition, 71 % were using some kind of gear to give the appearance of a penis, and 43 % were wearing a prosthetic penis.

Of the surgical interventions possible, chest surgery was privileged. Over half the group (51 %) had undergone chest surgery (reconstruction or reduction), 40 % had had a full mastectomy, and many discussed a desire to get such procedures done in the future. A significantly smaller portion (6 %) had had genital surgery, and only a few had gotten testicular implants. This reflected international findings that many FtMs in contemporary contexts did not engage in this modification but privileged hormonal treatments and chest surgery (Yerke and Mitchell 2011). Other elements to physical transition that participants reported engaging in included having a hysterectomy, engaging in weight lifting, pursuing diet and weight loss, getting masculine haircuts, having liposuction, having a cosmetic beard shadow

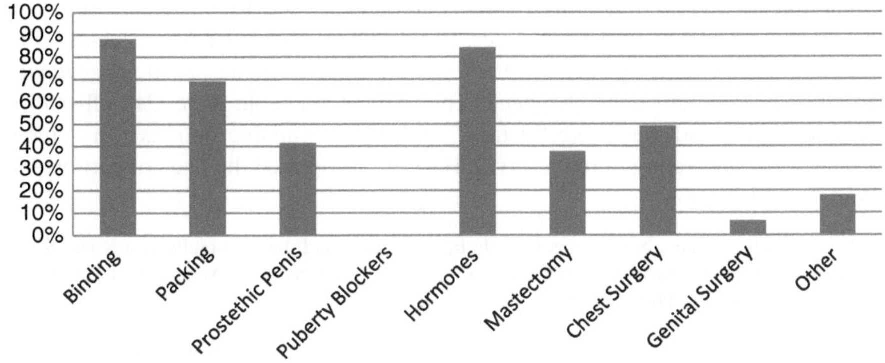

Fig. 5.1 Physical modifications the *E-males* participants have engaged in (n = 157)

applied (the look of facial hair), wearing male clothing, and wearing hip compression shorts (which slim the hips) (Fig. 5.1).

Overall, most participants expressed a level of comfort with, or at least acceptance of, their original genitalia (or front hole/boy hole as it was sometimes termed), explaining that top surgery and other forms of masculinisation were more important to them. Jon Snow (male/trans guy, 23 years) dreamed of what he termed a "real chest"—"*the flat kind with the pecks*". He expanded that whilst he *respected* guys who wanted a real penis, "*at the moment it's not in the plan*". He explained that he had a fiancé and would be spending his life with her, and he knew that she "*won't care what junk I have*". Jon concluded that overall he just wasn't interested in bottom surgery, particularly as he did not experience a huge amount of dysphoria around his genitals, enjoyed sex a lot, and had no desire to change how he had it. Ramir wanted a more masculine body overall, especially in terms of fat distribution, but was most keen to get (and had the least reservations about) chest surgery. He had invested in binding tops but had really spent very little thus far, and worried about the impacts of many treatments:

> I doubt I will ever get bottom surgery, although I do wish for a penis during sex, I am mostly ok with what's downstairs and don't feel the urge (bordering on desperation) like I do when considering top surgery. I also feel drawn to taking T but am worried about the permanence, and about being reliant on something (I'm a bit of a hippy that way I guess) (Ramir, transgender, 25 years).

Some participants did however express a strong desire to access genital surgery as a way to "complete" themselves. Darkneko (FtM transgender, 21 years) said, "*I intend to go for hormones and eventual SRS. I need to complete this journey*". Jay also explained:

> Although I know a penis doesn't make someone a man or not, for me it is something I have always wanted and felt I was missing. I plan to rectify that to enable me to feel whole and complete (Jay, male, 30 years).

Some of the participants had gone or were planning to go overseas to have phalloplasty as it was not accessible in Australia. Many participants also said they would like to access phalloplasty but were unable due to financial constraints or concerns about functional outcomes. For example, zbdsm (male, 57 years) said, "*I would love to do more such as phalloplasty, but the chances of me ever having the funds needed will never happen*". The options available were also off-putting for many, who said they were "scared" or that the available options were "meh" (a slang term suggesting unimpressive). Harry best captured the fears of participants about genital surgery:

> I want phallo or meta but there is so little info out there and the idea really scares me. So many surgeries to make it work, chances of failure, no sensation. Absolutely terrifying (Harry, FtM transgender, 24 years).

This comment summed up many reasons cited as to why genital surgery was less common, along with the fact that people had to travel to Serbia or Thailand to get it—where different health practice standards were in place.

Legal Transitions

Most male-identified participants had changed some kind of document to reflect their identity. Many other participants intended to change one or more document to reflect their name, a male sex or a neutral identity in the future. However, considering that this form of transition was less intrusive than surgery and only involved words on paper, changing documentation actually involved quite a few difficulties for most respondents. For some participants legal transitions were of high importance and represented an ultimate identity "goal", so such difficulties were traumatic. For example, Garfield (male, 31 years) had amended all his documents to reflect his male sex—including birth certificate, Australian and overseas passport, driver's license, healthcare (Medicare) card and so on. However he had moved interstate a few times whilst transitioning, and found that each state had different rules about what was required for recognition of gender and changing of documents. "*Having shifting goal posts made things quite challenging*", he commented. Jay (male, 30 years) had changed his name, driver's licence, birth certificate and passport over a period of years and after "*lots of running around certifying documents etc.*". But he felt that despite the difficulties it was important to him to have "*any paperwork I fill in from here on out reflect who I truly am*".

Aid (socially male, 18 years), found changing his documentation "*a hard and long process*" and his efforts were often met with resistance—some staff at Centrelink and Medicare[1] refused to do it. It was important to Aid to change his paperwork: "*mostly because I have been refused services due to photos that no longer look like me*".

---

[1] At the time anyone in Australia could change their name to a male name for example, but Medicare required proof of an irreversible medical sex change to "become male". As the report was being put together, this condition became more flexible due to the 2013 intervention of Federal Health Minister Tanya Plibersek.

He also felt that without the amendments, doing paperwork was "*a gamble*", because "*if your gender is in question it allows people to discriminate*". Doc79 (male, 33 years) changed his documentation both to reflect how he felt, and to be able to marry his wife and be named as father to their future children. However, when he changed his name at the bank the staff had an argument about whether he should be called a "Mr" or "Miss", because he hadn't changed his sex on his birth certificate yet (even though it was changed on other documents). It took a supervisor of the staff to intervene in the situation. Alex (transgender man/transman/transguy, 48 years) said he had particular difficulties in changing his passport, as he had been born outside of Australia, and it was a much more difficult process. He had sought legal advice, and managed to obtain the assistance of a gender representative by his side during meetings. The situation went to court, where he used proof of his Australian birth parents to eventually resolve the process. However, it required much patience, and reveals the need for legal advocates to be trained in gender identity issues, and the value of advocates who can assist and support transgender people during difficult legal battles.

Nikozilar (male, 20 years) changed his name the moment he turned 18, along with his driver's licence, bank details, electoral roll details, library card, passport and any other document possible. He was about to change his tax file info to "neutral", saying it was the best he could do at that stage, and that he yearned to be able to change his Medicare card and birth certificate but was unable to. He explained that not being able to get a document changed prevented him from engaging in situations where it needed to be used:

> Not being able to get my new Medicare card changed means that I'm shitting up my health – just because I hate being misgendered when I have to use my old Medicare card. I hate having any documents saying that I'm anything but male. I want everything changed so that no one can say otherwise.

The prerequisite for changing a Medicare card in Queensland, where he lived, was a hysterectomy. The Medicare office staff had at times rudely and loudly interrogated him over whether or not he'd had the surgery, which shamed him in that public space. Another time he was asked to submit lots of forms about the situation, but "*they never got back to me like they were going to... so depressing*".

Harry (FtM transgender, 24 years) had only changed a single document—his passport. Yet the (rural) post office he used to change it tried to charge him for the process, and didn't fill out the form properly. He had to go back to get the paperwork fixed. Whilst he felt such mistakes were understandable since changing sex on documentation "*isn't all that common*", he argued the postal clerks "*shouldn't have to rely on my knowledge of their job; they should be up to date with new information... actually, the passport policy had been in place for at least a year*". Whilst generally changing the sex markers on his documentation was secondary to Harry compared to how he looked, the process of getting his passport changed was important as he had to show it to someone for legal reasons and was "*going stealth*" (didn't want to out himself as having a transgender history). Name and sex change amendments were also sought by respondents at their schools and universities, on their rental agreements, on their gym memberships, on their video shop memberships and a range of other documents; with a mixture of positive and negative responses. It was clear that each time an amendment was made, the individual had to publicly out themselves as some variation of transgender, and so become placed in a vulnerable position (quite often in a public venue). Staff who gave affirming treatment and dealt with the process according to policies quickly and efficiently were greatly appreciated. But there were many who lacked discretion or knowledge about how to handle the situation overall.

Satisfaction with Transitioning

In a 10 point scale where participants were required to rate their current physical appearance from feminine (0) to masculine (10), the average number rated at a 7 (standard deviation 1.95, n = 182), suggesting they mainly felt they looked moderately masculine in the main. The minimum value was a 2, from a participant who had as yet been unable to access interventions, and the maximum value was 10, from participants who had generally engaged in much intervention. The survey data showed that the overwhelming majority of participants (97 %) said that the physical modifications they engaged in made a difference to their lives and 78 % were satisfied with the results (ranging from very to somewhat satisfied). This satisfaction often related to hormones and chest surgery. For example, thewaywesee (trans* male or queer male, 22 years) said he was very satisfied since starting hormones; calling the treatment "*One of the best decisions I've ever made*". Garfield (male, 31 years) was satisfied with his chest surgery, commenting that whilst he could not walk around bare-chested ("*scars too obvious on my lily-white skin and I'm not all that hairy*"), he now had a masculine silhouette. "*People who meet me now have no idea that I haven't always looked this way*". Bearcooking (male, 58 years) was very satisfied with his chest reconstruction, total hysterectomy, oophorectomy, vaginoplasty, scrotal formation and implants, and metoidioplasty. He was also happy with the impacts of taking testosterone regularly in the form of deep muscle depot injection.

A smaller 8 % were neutral on the outcome, 8 % were somewhat dissatisfied, 3 % were dissatisfied, and only 1 % were very dissatisfied. There was a general reluctance to express dissatisfaction, and it tended to be related to complications from surgical interventions. zbdsm (male, 57 years) said, "*If I'm being honest with myself, I'd say I'm less satisfied than I'd like to be*", but that he generally doesn't give his qualms a thought. He explained that he had had male chest reconstruction twice as the first doctor was "*too incompetent to know simple math*". He did not like having his shirt off around strangers because despite being skillful, the second doctor simply couldn't fix the location of his nipples, and the way his "*areolas are somewhat elongated in an outward/downward direction*". Doc79 (male, 33 years) similarly said, "*chest recon left me badly scarred and yet my surgeon's response was: 'Oh well, your hair will cover it'*". Nipple reconstruction was necessary as there was little left, and he'd had complications with phalloplasty. He commented,

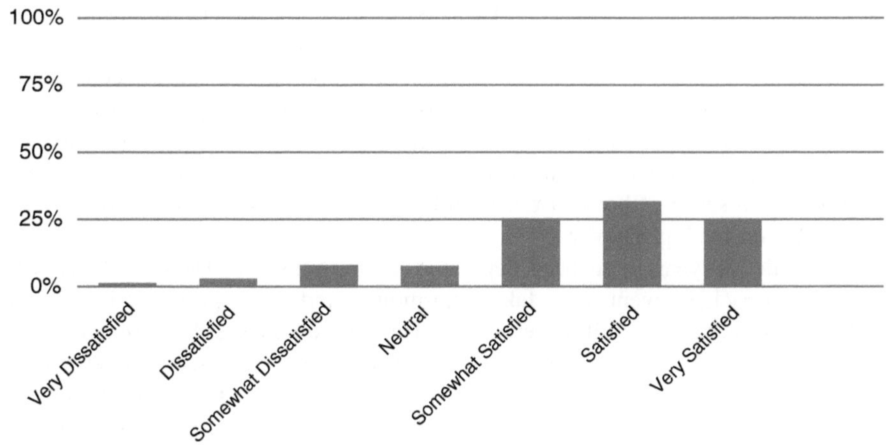

Fig. 5.2 *E-males'* level of satisfaction with physical interventions (n = 155)

"*I wish I had waited till I could afford better surgeons... but what I got is better than what I had pre-surgery*". There were also cases where testosterone had impacted the voices of singers specifically, changing the tone and limiting the range of their voices in ways they did not like. They wished they had been warned about that danger. There are methods that lower (but do not eliminate) the risk of this occurring—starting with a lower dose of testosterone, and gradually increasing this over time (more akin to a physiological puberty) (Fig. 5.2).

Impact on Wellbeing

The participants asserted that there was, in their experience, a direct relationship between transitioning and a reduction in mental health disorders and an increased general sense of well-being. For example, Harry (FtM transgender, 24 years) had suffered from anxiety prior to transition, and was taking prescription medication for this diagnosis. However, he said that his transition thus far involved a combination of changing his body through taking hormones for two years and working out at the gym, and changing his look through using binders, packers and a prosthetic. He had started getting a masculine haircut and wearing clothes. He had also changed his name. For Harry, a major goal of transitioning was to pass as male socially, so whilst he would still like to get chest surgery and feels he has certainly had to "settle" for lower quality packers than he would like, this overall aim is being achieved. He said that the combination of transition processes he has been able to access thus far had made a "*massive difference*", and commented "*I now pass and I'm off my anxiety meds*".

Conor (male, queer, trans*, person of colour, 24 years), had been diagnosed with an eating disorder prior to transition. His transition consisted of taking testosterone for a year and getting chest surgery. He said that the chest surgery had meant he no longer needed to bind his chest, which "*has improved my sense of freedom and embodiment*". For Conor, the major goal of transitioning was about becoming at peace with the look of his body, and did not require bottom surgery to achieve the overall masculine aesthetic he aimed at. The changes from both testosterone and top surgery have "*helped me to deal with my ED (eating disorder)*", and whilst occasionally a sense of body criticism did arise he had come a long way in overcoming it and feeling happier.

Jay (male, 30 years) had been depressed before transition. He started out with binders and packers, went on to taking hormones, and in the past year had gotten both chest surgery and a full hysterectomy. He reported he was "*very satisfied with the results*", despite the need for a revision on his chest and a desire to get bottom surgery. For Jay, the concept of transition was about being able to feel whole and complete, rectifying his body and correcting what he experienced as missing. The transition processes he had engaged in so far had "*made a massive difference to my life*". Jay said:

> I feel more at home in my own skin that I ever have. I have more confidence and I am more outgoing and generally more into living my life rather than just existing as I was prior to transitioning.

Aid (socially male, 18 years), had been suicidal as a young person, before his transition. He had been having testosterone injections for three years since he was 15, and had recently gotten chest surgery. For Aid, the main point of transition was to make his life bearable—to increase his comfort within himself and when naked. He was fairly satisfied, and although he wished for no scars he realised that it was impossible to achieve. Regardless, he said the surgery and testosterone had completely changed how he felt: "*I feel less anxiety and hate towards myself*". The problems he had were all now "social" in nature—related to other people's reactions to him and transphobia, rather than his own reactions to himself. "*I feel at peace with my body,*" he explained, "*and I am no longer suicidal*". He was considering getting a hysterectomy, a metoidioplasty and phalloplasty in the future, "*so I can live without the fear of ovarian cancer and so I can feel more comfortable naked in change rooms and with doctors*".

Doc79 (male, 33 years) had both anxiety and depression before his transition. He had started out with getting a haircut, and then started hormone therapy, "*which moved fat deposits around and lowered my voice, and made me incredibly hairy like a bear*". He then had a series of surgeries: a full hysterectomy, oophorectomy, mastectomy (chest reconstruction), nipple reconstruction, metoidioplasty with urethra extension, and finally went overseas to get a phalloplasty because it was not available in Australia. For Doc79, transitioning meant physically manifesting his male identity so that he could just feel like what he termed a "normal" man. Whilst there were complications, he still preferred his body now to how it had been earlier, and reflected:

> Most people after a mastectomy (which was my first surgical intervention) are in pain, bedridden. After mine I went out to my family's house to play cards, drains hanging around

> and all! I had never felt more normal, more alive than the day after that mastectomy. Even now, with the scars, I am more normal than with what I was born with.

He said that whilst he still gets some anxiety, "*I have never had depression since the day I admitted I had GID and started the process of transitioning... I'll never regret it*".

Costs of Transitioning

Participants had spent a range of amounts of money on transitioning, ranging from nothing to over $100,000. The largest group (28 %) invested between $5,000 and $10,000. The second largest group (20 %) had spent between $1,000 and $5,000, 19 % had spent between $10,000 and $30,000, 18 % had spent between $200 and $1,000. It was less common to have spent smaller or larger amounts: only 5 % of the participants paid less than $200; and only 5 % had spent over $30,000 (including 1 % who had spent over $100,000 in their transition) (Fig. 5.3).

At the lower end of the price scale, Draconem (FtM transgender, 24 years) wore a binder that cost about $60, and said "*that's all I can afford right now*". He also had some new jeans from his dad for his birthday, and clothes donated by other people, and a $30 haircut. He was not completely satisfied, but even with this relatively smaller amount spent had made him more positive about his life. Financial issues prevented him from getting a packer, engaging in hormone therapy or seeking surgery. *Lance* (male/transsexual male, 40 years) had spent around $200 on a binder, packer, clothing and workouts. These things gave him "*more confidence in myself*" and made him feel supported, and were "*the things necessary to feel and appear masculine while waiting for surgery*". He intended to have top

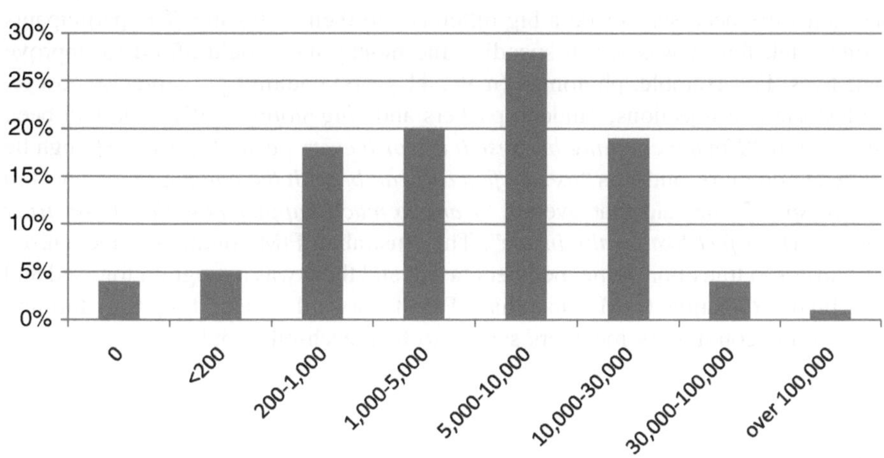

Fig. 5.3 Money invested by *E-males* participants in the transition process (n = 157)

surgery, but was taking his time to get the best options financially and for his wellbeing. Jon Snow had spent around $500—purchasing masculine clothing and haircuts, not shaving, binding and going to the gym three times a week. He was pleased with how muscular he had become, and his mannerisms had naturally evolved from having brothers as he grew up. "*Money wise, I don't really see it as investing, more just living. I am just happy I got the ball rolling,*" he reflected. He was happier by far and looking forward to his future. Maddox (male/ftm/transman, 21 years) had spent around $1,000 on sports, working out, dressing masculine, wearing multiple sports bras at once or binders, an STP, and taking T. He was saving for top surgery as binding his chest was frustrating—he was not a big guy but had a big chest which led to a fair bit of dysphoria. He noted that the fact that transitioning was possible at all "*has me too grateful to complain too much*", and believed "*this is the happiest and most honest I've ever been*". He saw himself considering bottom surgery if the outcomes could fit his desired standards of function and form.

At the higher end of the price scale, Jay (male, 30 years) said he had spent at least $15,000 and was very satisfied with what it had bought. He had started out with binders ($30–$40 each) and packers ($15–$50 each depending on if they were STP enabled or not), and had been on hormones since 2009 at $140 every 12 weeks. In the past year he had undergone chest surgery ($10k) and a full hysterectomy (at cost to him on the public health system). Bearcooking (male, 58 years) had spent close to $100,000 on top and bottom surgeries, and testosterone deep muscle depot injections, and was investing in further lower surgery. He was also very satisfied overall, as were all participants who had spent higher amounts. Several participants made jokes about wanting to win the lottery in order to do more. It was clear that whilst money spent certainly did not guarantee a "perfect" result, and some people did not want to engage in costly (or any) treatments purely because they were simply not part of their transition or self-affirmation plan—having access to the funds necessary to support the particular changes the participant felt *were* necessary made a big difference to their wellbeing. The participants strongly felt that it was worth spending the money they could afford to improve their lives. For example, photoman (male, 41 years) couldn't put a precise cost on the testosterone injections, binders, packers and "*big sloppy clothes*" he had been investing in: "*I'm not counting because it is worth every penny I spend*". Though he wanted to do more, and was "*as satisfied as I can be with the amount of money I am able to spend*", he said that overall, "*I am so much happier now that I can truly portray who I feel like on the inside*". The Australian FtM community recognised the barriers to transition some members faced, and there was a program for used and new binder donation (FtM Australia's Pay-it-Forward Binder Program) through which some community members sought to help each-other out.

Problems and Temptations

Despite the anonymity of the study, no participant reported having broken the law, engaged in the black market, or having used unapproved treatments or someone else's prescriptions. A few said that they had been tempted. They cited financial issues and accessibility (particularly denial of access to hormones) as the main motivator. However, safety concerns about the potential impacts of buying unmonitored online hormones had prevented the respondents from doing so. There was also a sense that the respondents had worked hard on their bodies, and did not want to damage them through low quality products that did not fit Australian standards. They also indicated that their wariness about what hormones they used was a sign of maturity and life experience. Like most participants, zbdsm (male, 57 years) said he would never consider using unmonitored hormones, or a prescription or medication belonging to anyone else, reflecting, "maybe it's because I'm older, maybe it's because I know better".

There were reports of specific legal difficulties for younger Transgender FtM people in the study. For young people there was the option of going on puberty blockers, which could halt their development of secondary sex characteristics (menstruation, breast development), and in some cases it was possible to seek approval for hormone therapy or even chest surgery. But there was a requirement to go through family courts to seek such treatments—even if they had the support of parents or guardians to pursue them. For example, when Aid was a young teen of 15 years, he had experienced difficulties in seeking to get hormone therapy; he was not allowed to start the treatment before seeing a psychologist, "who put me on a 6 month waiting list". Despite his youth, he had actually already been waiting for years to start his transition, but had not begun purely due to his fear of publicly coming forward and the social issues it could cause him. So in that period he said, "I considered accessing black market T". A few younger FtMs facing legal and financial obstacles to their transitions, and those who were otherwise in lower socio-economic demographics or had less access to services for other reasons, mentioned that they had considered taking black market hormone options out of sheer desperation.

There were also reports of particular difficulties for genderqueer people, who wished to actualise a sense of themselves as neither female nor male by manifesting this more directly in their embodiment, around accessing transition-related treatments. Hansel (genderqueer, age 22 years) explained that he had personally not faced obstacles as a genderqueer person in this regard; he was supported by his psychologist to express himself more through accessing testosterone treatment—which had been on for one month, within a set of self-actualisation processes that included binding and more masculine clothing, and experimenting with various hairstyles short and long. However, he had certainly been approached by other genderqueer people wishing to share his testosterone prescription. He said they approached him because, "the whole process is pretty daunting and some psychologists are reluctant to give T to people who identify as genderqueer". He explained that there were many stories online on genderqueer discussion-boards and groups about bad treatment, “so some people are afraid to go through the process for themselves”. It was clear there was a need for service-providers to have a better understanding of the needs of genderqueer people and the ways they may engage in treatments. There was also a need for services to show that they were “genderqueer friendly” so that people could feel safe to access them, rather than to seek treatment through a friend or online acquaintance out of fear.

Chapter 6
Health

Abstract This chapter discusses data on health generated by the 273 FtM transgender Australians in the 2013 *E-Males* study. Participants mainly considered their physical health in the past year to have been good or very good. Unfortunately, they reported that many of the health service-providers they had used, such as doctors, had a lack of knowledge about transgender issues. There were reports of doctors making offensive statements and misgendering patients. The participants often found themselves having to "educate" health-care practitioners due to gaps in their education on transgender issues. There was a lack of transgender healthcare services in rural areas, so some participants travelled long distances to access treatment. Participants greatly valued health-care providers who educated themselves on transgender issues, were friendly, treated them in accordance with their gender identity and arranged assistance from other services that they required. Some participants did not disclose their transgender identity to their health-care providers.

Keywords Transgender · FtM · Health · Physical · Medical · Doctor · Nurse · Education · Knowledge · Care

> Life in general is pretty good. I think the best things would be where I live, and the fact I can take photographs whenever I want. I suppose about the only thing I would change would be having enough money to be able to get surgeries done. Overall I am pretty happy with who I am, although there are certain aspects I would like to change, like decreasing the amount of drinking I do and cut back on the ciggies (photoman, male, 41 years).

> My experiences have been good with doctors in Melbourne. Doctors in my area (rural vic) have little to no knowledge of trans healthcare. I am educating them and I am not comfortable with this. So at home, healthcare is terrible. Good experiences has been welcoming doctors, one of which allows me to communicate via email so that I don't have to travel over two hours to see them. They are also assisting me to find a good local GP. Bad experiences have been doctors who just don't care, have no idea about trans healthcare and ask me to basically tell them what my medical plan should be. They make me feel uncomfortable. I would like to see it become easier for rural trans people to get adequate healthcare. I only found my good GP and psychiatrist because I got lucky and found

T. Jones et al., *Female-to-Male (FtM) Transgender People's Experiences in Australia*, SpringerBriefs in Sociology, DOI 10.1007/978-3-319-13829-9_6

someone who is trans who put me on to them. It is very hard to find fellow trans people in these areas and there is no visibility of a community existing in other areas either. There needs to be more services visible, so you don't need to out yourself while you are looking for help (Harry, FtM transgender, 24 years).

Key Findings

- In the main, participants considered their physical health to have been good or very good in the past year.
- Health service-providers had a lack of knowledge about transgender issues.
- There was a unanimous agreement among participants about the need for health-care practitioners to have greater education on transgender issues.
- The participants find themselves having to "educate" their doctors.
- There was a lack of availability and/or visibility of transgender healthcare services in rural areas.
- "Misgendering" of *E-males* participants by health service-providers negatively impacted the treatment experience for these patients.

Physical Health

When asked how they would describe their physical health in the past 12 months, 62 % answered in an affirming manner (45 % said it was good and 17 % said it was very good). This was similar to the findings for the general transgender population in *Tranznation* (Couch et al. 2007). A further 23 % answered that it was neither good nor bad. A smaller group of 14 % said that it was bad, and less than 1 % said it was very bad. For many of the participants, going to the gym had been a key part of affirming their gender identity or their chosen transition path in the last year, as being more muscular (whether that meant becoming larger or in some cases smaller in overall size) was part of their ideal vision for their body. Several participants attributed becoming more involved in weight lifting programs (formal or informal), doing sports or exercise, and paying extra attention to their bodies as improving their physical fitness and health. Conversely, there was a smaller group of participants who felt they needed to lose a bit of weight as it was causing them physical discomfort when binding for example, whilst for one man his weight had exacerbated his arthritis (Fig. 6.1).

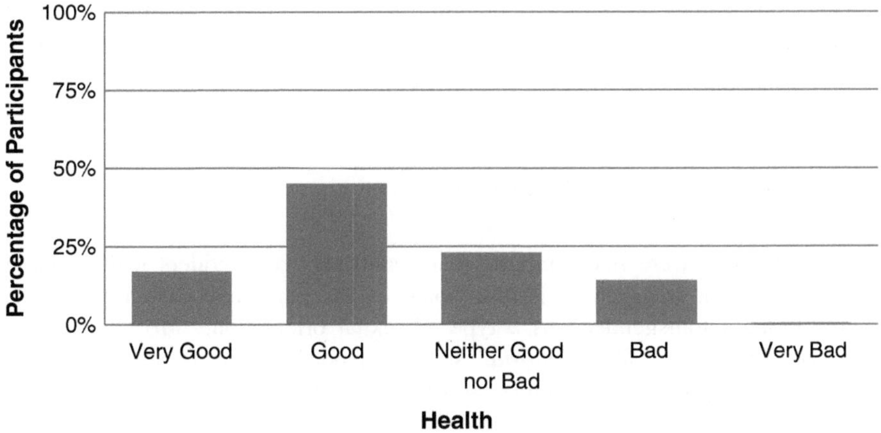

Fig. 6.1 Health of *E-males* participants in the last year (n = 223)

Alcohol and Drug Use

We asked the participants about their use of alcohol, cigarettes and a range of drugs (from marijuana to heroin). Most of the participants mentioned that they consumed alcohol at least occasionally (33 %), monthly (8 %), fortnightly (12 %), weekly (21 %) or daily (8 %). Almost one fifth never drank. Over half of the respondents never smoked, whilst around one fifth of the group smoked daily. The majority of the *E-males* participants never used any other drugs, and no participant used heroin. About one fifth of the group smoked marijuana on occasion, 5 % used it daily, 3 % weekly. A group of 15 % occasionally used sedatives such as sleeping pills, and a few individuals used them more often. There was almost negligible regular use of all other drugs, with some participants using them only on occasion (11 % used ecstasy occasionally, 7 % used amphetamines occasionally, 5 % used cocaine occasionally, and 2 % used inhalants occasionally).

Of the few participants who discussed having addiction issues, Harleyguy (transsexual male, 40 years) explained how these issues were intertwined with his difficulty in accepting his gender identity and other complications:

> Mental health is a fine line for me. I am bipolar and ADHD with addiction issues. I actually self-medicated for years… the same substance I was addicted to is now my prescribed medication and I have never functioned better! A number of people have commented that I was a self-medicator. A lot was tied up also with transgender issues; I was at my worst addiction-wise when I fell in love with a gay man and it made me realise that I was transgender (instead of repressing it), and possibly a gay one at that. I was in a lesbian relationship at the time, so this was a total flip of the coin for me and it exacerbated mental health issues.

Other individuals related their addiction issues to childhood trauma, or a combination of mental health issues that they believed heightened their susceptibility to substance abuse.

Bad Experiences with Health Services

In general, there were many reports that health service-providers had a lack of knowledge about transgender issues. Some of the participants even found that people thought transgender was a type of sexual orientation. "*Most have never heard of trans* or gender dysphoria,*" said Aid (socially male, 18 years), who had experienced only two good doctors out of eight he had been to. Aid had actually had a doctor say to him that she "*hated treating trans people,*" and he suspected another treated him purely out of curiosity to "*get a look at my body*". He recalled times he had tried to explain his identity to a doctor for over 40 min and had then been asked if he was a "hermaphrodite". He had also experienced a doctor who refused to write him a script "*because he didn't know what I was*", and had even had a doctor who was "*so shocked he was unable to type 'testosterone' into his computer for a script*"—to the point where the session had to end and he had to go back to a different doctor in the clinic that same day.

Doc79 (male, 33 years) had experienced a doctor who was so uninformed that they were "*acting like I was the first person on earth that had ever done this*", as well as a doctor who seemed to be in a state of genuine shock and said they "*had no idea*" how to deal with him. However, the fall-out of these experiences was not simply an awkward interaction or a lack of aid; Doc79 reported having to change endocrinologists, as the first one had such a bad grasp on the hormonal needs of FtM transgender people and had been experimenting with dosages. As a consequence Doc79 was still trying to adjust his testosterone levels with the assistance of a new doctor. Several participants talked about doing research online, talking to people "on the grapevine" or outing themselves early on in their engagement with health practitioners in order to find out which health practitioners had knowledge of transgender issues, and avoid those who did not. Bad experiences with health service-providers also involved "*having to educate them and having to deal with being misgendered*" (Conor, male, queer, trans*, person of colour, 24 years). It appeared that this also occurred in specialized services:

> The worst would have to be the *(Gender identity)* Clinic calling me and confirming my appointment with my birth name even though I had previously given them my preferred name and it was written down in their diary. I called the receptionist/nurse out on why she used my birth name and she was really rude about it as if I should know that it wasn't her fault that I was upset; that it was my fault to hope they of all health-care professionals would be respectful (Maddox, male/ftm/transman, 21 years).

Analysis of the participants' experiences revealed that geographical location was a decisive factor in terms of accessibility and quality of health services. Harry (FtM transgender, 24 years) contrasted the differences across his state of Victoria, saying that his best experiences were with doctors and health-care providers in the city area of Melbourne. In contrast, doctors in his rural home area "*have little to no knowledge of trans* healthcare*". Like many of the participants who mentioned having poorly prepared providers, he was providing them with what little educational information he could. But he was not comfortable with this, and felt that the situation was terrible:

> I would like to see it become easier from rural trans* people to get adequate healthcare. I only found my good GP and psychiatrist because I got lucky and found someone who is trans* who put me on to them. It is very hard to find fellow trans* people in these areas and there is no visibility of a community existing in other areas either. There needs to be more services visible, so you don't need to out yourself while you are looking for help.

Photoman (male, 41 years) lived in a rural area and found he had to travel for four and a half hours just to see a doctor he could trust. The alternative was to deal with incompetent practitioners whom he had to teach:

> … the locals I do not trust or like. Most of the time they are locums and I was continually having to tell them what was happening with my treatment. The locums at my local centre have no idea and do not understand trans* issues. My regular GP has some knowledge and has been educating himself on trans* issues and treatments, that's why I prefer to travel.

There were quite a few participants who had this issue, and there was a clear need for more education of rural health providers.

Good Experiences with Health Services

In describing good experiences with health service-providers, participants mentioned their contact with "friendly" doctors who facilitated other avenues of communication and access to care. Harry (FtM transgender, 21 years) said his best experiences were with welcoming doctors, including one who "*allows me to communicate via email so that I don't have to travel over two hours to see them*" and who was assisting him to find a good local GP. Doc79 fondly recalled one doctor who was particularly friendly and helpful in the early stages of transition:

> He used to arm wrestle me after he gave me my T shot, to see if I had any hormone induced strength… He used to let me win I think, but it was good because he was one of my first docs and it was at the start of my transition, so it was good for a laugh at a rough time.

There were other descriptions of doctors who called 20 psychologists until they found the one that would help their patient towards getting hormone therapy, and doctors who were affirming of their patients. Gestures of warmth and acceptance were greatly appreciated by the participants, as were practitioners who had knowledge and understanding, and familiarity with treating FtM people.

Other participants reported that being treated by doctors who had previously treated other transgender people was a positive factor. Nikozilar (male, 20 years) was very satisfied with his "*extremely open minded and friendly*" GP, and particularly noted that she had "*treated trans* men and trans women before*". He recounted that she referred him to other services and practitioners, performed regular pap-smears on him to check his health, taught his partner "very patiently" how to give him hormone shots, and "*always referred to me as he*". Maddox (male/ftm/transman, 21 years) argued that younger health-care professionals who had lived, worked and studied in "big Western cities" had a fairly strong basis of what transgender is compared to those who were older or were mainly based in rural areas. He also felt it impacted their knowledge of terms like "*gender dysphoria and gender neutral*". For Jake (male, 21 years) and others being treated in a way that was consistent with their gender identity was of paramount importance. He said that when he had his hysterectomy as a public patient in a public hospital, there was "not one slip up of male pronouns or being treated as male". He appreciated that he was even "*offered a urinal bottle (for men obviously) but I simply just stated I would prefer to get up and walk to the bathroom*". He also appreciated when service-providers were willing to research issues that they did not have all the necessary knowledge on:

> My GP and the Sexual Health clinic are great. They sometimes lack a bit of knowledge but are more than happy to look it up or find out for me etc. I am not the only trans* person they treat. They have a general understanding but it is not their area of expertise like say an endocrinologist, but they do have one of those on staff who visits from time to time.

Other Lessons for Health Service-Providers

Some of the key lessons for health service-providers to emerge from the data were the need to learn about transgender identities. Particularly, to understand that transgender is not a sexual orientation, that gender identity can be complex and that FtM transgender people are a different group to MtF Transgender people (about whom there is more information). Another key point was that FtM transgender people needed early and consistent support and affirmation for any disclosure of their identity, even if it was still being determined. Saying "it would be okay if you turned out to be transgender" is not saying "you are transgender" or foreclosing on the patient's identity.

Some of the patients were out as transgender or as having a transgender past to their health practitioners, but not all were. For example, Darkneko (FtM transgender, 21 years) said, "*I never informed any of my doctors of my trans status. One time I was wearing my binder and the doctor saw but didn't say anything*". Having supportive posters or displays (even a rainbow flag or transgender flag sticker), or information available on gender identity in the treatment space could communicate that the patient is safe to discuss their gender identity with service workers in a non-intimidating way. Maddox, Conor and many other participants argued for more education to be put in place so that there were better health-care services for the transgender community and to redress these issues. Conor suggested health-care services should have “preferred name and pronouns” on all their admission sheets. Other suggestions by the participants included the need for health services purely for FtM transgender people, and the need for Australian practitioners and surgeons who specialised in performing surgeries for FtM transitions, including bottom surgery (in which experts are currently only found overseas).

Chapter 7
Mental Health

Abstract This chapter describes data on mental health generated by the 273 FtM transgender Australians in the 2013 *E-Males* study. Whilst most participants were satisfied with their lives in general, a high proportion (69 %) had received a diagnosis of depression and anxiety within the previous 12 months. Over 80 % of the participants had thought about self-harm or suicide. Over two thirds had self-harmed and over one third had attempted suicide. The group mostly attributed their wellbeing risks to their personal issues in regards to their trans* identity or gender dysphoria; other issues included experiences of transphobia. Many participants related improvements in mental health to processes of coming out or transitioning. The participants had used a range of mental health service providers from general psychologists through to gender identity experts. They preferred experienced, affirming gender-focussed providers who offered streamlined processes and ongoing support. They expressed concerns about expensive, disinterested and judgemental service-providers.

Keywords Transgender · FtM · Mental health · Suicide · Self-harm · Depression · Dysphoria · Psychologist · Counsellor · Gender identity expert

> I'm really happy with how my life is going, especially since coming out as trans. I still struggle with my mental health, I've always had very low downs that can feel debilitating, so I am continuing therapy and considering medication. I am often lacking in sex drive for long periods of time, but that could be due to depression and being busy. Otherwise my life is really great. I have wonderful friends and care for rescue dogs, I have a kind and understanding partner, a great and satisfying job and enough money to get by (most of the time anyway). I wish I could feel a bit more stable and enjoy more drive (whether it be for work, creativity or sex) but I am working on that and am lucky to have great support. I feel very positive about my future, and am lucky to have had some great opportunities arise in my music career in the past year. I'm very proud of how far I have come, and the huge struggles that I have gotten through. Looking back, I'm just proud to still be here today! (Sam, transgender, 25 years).

> I went to counselling through ACON and I came across a trans guy. He runs a support group which is brilliant. I've been to a psychiatrist to get my diagnosis in order to transition. ACON is great – supportive, informative (VB, transsexual male, 32 years).

T. Jones et al., *Female-to-Male (FtM) Transgender People's Experiences in Australia*, SpringerBriefs in Sociology, DOI 10.1007/978-3-319-13829-9_7

Key Findings

- Most participants were at least somewhat satisfied with their lives in general.
- A very high proportion (69 %) of participants had received a diagnosis of depression and anxiety within the previous 12 months.
- Participants largely attributed their very high rates of self-harm, suicidal ideation and suicide attempts and to their personal issues in regards to their trans* identity. They also cited other issues, and experiences of transphobia.
- In the blogs, many of the participants partly related their mental health problems to gender dysphoria. They often related improvements in mental health to the process of coming out about their gender identity, and the process of transitioning.
- Participants commented on the lack of GLBTIQ supports in rural areas.

Life Satisfaction and Wellbeing

Overall, a majority of 63 % of the *E-males* respondents were satisfied with their lives in general (10 % felt neutral about their lives and 26 % were dissatisfied). Of those who were satisfied, the comments tended to focus on the sense that self-acceptance had improved their life. For example, one participant said, "*10 out of 10. I feel I have been true to myself regardless of fear and challenges*", and several others reflected on how things were steadily improving and how they had much to look forward to now that they knew who they were. On the other hand, Draconem (FtM transgender, 24 years) was dissatisfied, and said "*I wish I could have been born a boy, but don't we all*". He also yearned for more money to get a packer/STP and medical treatments. Whilst things were improving with his transition, he said that "*at the end of the day, when I take off my binder and I'm naked before the mirror* (*after my shower*)... I just get depressed". He said he found himself wondering "*what the point of it all is if that's what I have to see every day*". Several other participants who were dissatisfied with their lives expressed that they were impatient around achieving particular gender milestones or hated the sight of themselves naked (Fig. 7.1).

When it came to specific areas of their lives, the results were not as strong as they were for general life satisfaction. For example, regarding their jobs/studies, 56 % of the respondents were satisfied (9 % felt neutral about their jobs/studies and 35 % were dissatisfied). The qualitative data suggested that satisfaction was closely tied to having a supportive work/study environment, enough money to live comfortably and a focus on an area of interest. For example, photoman (male, 41 years) commented that he was content with the focus of his life, "*I can take photographs whenever I want*", but he wished he could have more money to be able to get surgeries done. Regarding their physical health, 53 % of the respondents were satisfied (14 % felt neutral about their physical health and 32 % were dissatisfied).

Level of satisfaction with	Very Dissatisfied	Dissatisfied	Somewhat Dissatisfied	Neutral	Somewhat Satisfied	Satisfied	Very Satisfied	N
your life in general?	7%	7%	12%	10%	20%	32%	11%	220
your social life?	7%	7%	18%	14%	18%	28%	9%	220
your romantic life?	11%	13%	8%	14%	11%	21%	22%	219
your sexual life?	12%	18%	15%	18%	9%	15%	13%	218
your physical health?	5%	11%	16%	14%	24%	22%	7%	219
your job/studies?	11%	9%	15%	9%	19%	22%	15%	220

Fig. 7.1 Life satisfaction of *E-males* participants

To improve physical health, most people comments were on the desire to lose weight, gain muscle, drink less or cut back on cigarettes.

Regarding relationships, the results similarly showed only a slight trend towards satisfaction. In regards to their social life generally, a majority of 55 % of the respondents were satisfied (14 % felt neutral about their social lives and 32 % were dissatisfied). Most of the participants responding positively spoke of having one or more good friends. Several of those who were dissatisfied expressed feeling "behind" in terms of male socialisation and male friendships. Regarding their romantic life, a majority of 54 % of the respondents were satisfied (14 % felt neutral about their romantic lives and 32 % were dissatisfied). Those who were satisfied discussed having loving partners or enjoyable dates for example. The respondents were less satisfied with their sexual lives: only 37 % of the respondents were satisfied, 18 % felt neutral and a majority of 45 % were dissatisfied. There were mainly comments on the need for "*More sex!*", but also comments by people who did not enjoy sex generally and for whom frequency of sex would not be an improvement. For some the issue was with the quality of what could be achieved in their experience; there were participants who wanted an erectile device or wished for greater sensation in their penis after bottom surgery. As was often the case with difficult topics, several participants had a sense of humour about their dissatisfaction with their sex lives, and one participant joked; "*Thank god for the internet;) LOL*". Another joked, "*once my sex life ever gets off the ground I shall let you all know*".

zbdsm (male, 57 years) went into some detail on the discussion board about his life satisfaction, and illustrated how different parts of the participants' lives could have varied impacts on their wellbeing. He felt his job, romantic life and sexual life were impacting his wellbeing negatively. He had been a self-employed sub-contractor for the past 11 years until very recently and not earning much. This meant he was unable to take holidays, "*so I don't go anywhere and I don't do anything*". He found his life to be quite mundane, and said that subsequently at times he was quite depressed by it, "*everything is so-so, doing the same things every day, every month, every year*". He said he was aware that part of his depression was directly related to his age; he felt that although he was nearing 60 he had let himself down "*by not succeeding at anything in particular*", including completing all his desired surgeries, having a partner or going anywhere overseas. However, his life was somewhat improved by the fact that he had a good social life more broadly. He had some true friends and some loving, attentive family:

> I love my mate for what he gives to my life, which is as much as a friend can. Yet that too isn't enough to keep the ugly head of depression at bay... What I do though is try and see the positives and just keep on plodding on, because there are good things in my life; like having my daughter and her family around and caring for me, watching my grandsons grow up and having the best, best mate anyone could have... as well as some very long term friendships, including one of 53 years.

Mental Health Diagnoses

Most of the *E-males* survey participants (79 %) reported being diagnosed with depression and anxiety in the previous 12 months, which was higher than in previous Australian studies of the broader transgender population (Couch et al. 2007; Pitts et al. 2006). In addition, some respondents had received other mental health diagnoses: 14 % reported a diagnosis of post-traumatic stress disorder, 10 % reported a diagnosis of body dysmorphic disorder, 9 % reported a diagnosis of obsessive compulsive disorder, 6 % reported a diagnosis of borderline personality disorder and 6 % reported an eating disorder diagnosis. Other answers reported diagnoses of bipolar disorder and gender dysphoria (Fig. 7.2).

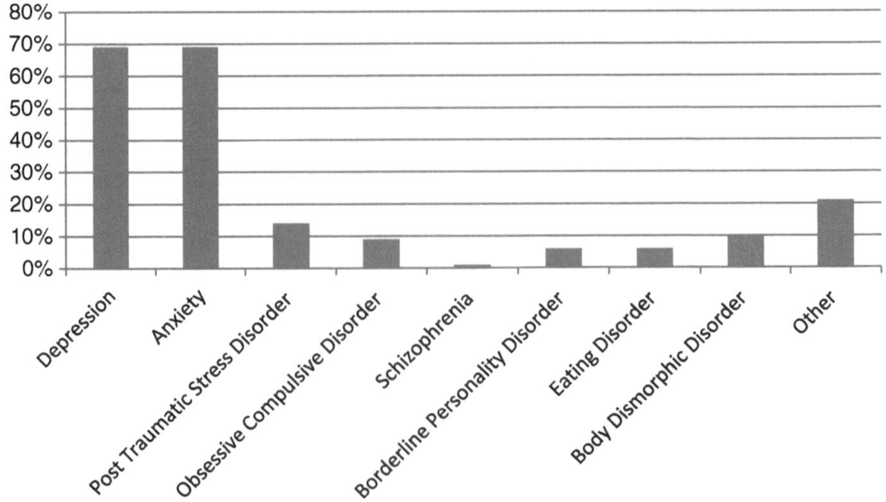

Fig. 7.2 Mental health disorders of *E-male participants* in the last 12 months (n = 127)

Gender identity—particularly when it could not be expressed fully—was understood by participants as a contributing factor for depression and anxiety. Draconem (FtM transgender, 24 years) said he got depressed occasionally, usually at night, and had been diagnosed with depression and social anxiety. "*These issues have arisen due to family problems (abuse), and self-ostracising, and in part gender identity*," he explained. Harleyguy (transsexual male, 40 years) explained that his addiction problems and mental health issues were at their worst when he was first coming to terms with being transgender. Eric (FtM transgender, age 49 years) commented: "*I have depression and anxiety (pattern here, huh?) and probably have had for a very long time, my doctor said*". He explained he would be permanently on medication, which helped, as he would "*go rather screwy without it*". Eric was not happy most of the time, but struggled with ways to change that. When he found out he might be transgender he said he did feel happier for a while, but his story illustrated how the wellbeing of many FtM Australians could be mediated by the achievement of, and barriers to, their gender milestones:

> When I got the guts to change my name at last, from a distinctly feminine to an androgynous one (based on my second name) I felt really good. Wearing guy clothes, the same. I found a menswear shop which made no fuss about me trying things on, even suggested I do so, and that made me feel great. But the good feelings don't last. I want top surgery and to be seen as male, but I don't have money. There seems to be no services, no gender clinics in this state. My doctor was sympathetic, when I finally got up the guts to tell her, but she doesn't know much about it either. If I could be happy without being transgender, that would be great, but I don't think I can.

Many participants said that being able to express their gender to a greater extent—whether through transition or other affirmations of self—was associated with improvements to their mental health. *Harry* (FtM transgender, 24 years) commented that although he had previously been diagnosed with social anxiety and depression he was "*doing pretty well, basically since I started passing (as a man) full time*". He had been off his medication for two years, and whilst he still occasionally got depressed it was not related to his own feelings about his gender anymore, but to his lack of a social life (due to a high study load and the fact he lived in a rural area with no GLBTIQ community). He said, "*I'm happier than I ever remember being in my life (since passing as male)*". *Brett* (male/transgender male, 27 years) had previously been diagnosed with schizophrenia, anxiety and depression; but explained that he'd been extremely stable for years since transitioning: "*…my mental illness stems a lot from the root of gender dysphoria, so transitioning has made an amazing impact on staying well*". Jay (male, 30 years) had been diagnosed with adjustment disorder with reactive depression and anxiety. This meant that generally after high stress situations or life-altering events, he would get depressed and "*feel lost and generally washed out*". But he was surprised to find that he had no such symptoms after transition processes such as surgeries. Maddox (male/ftm/transman, 21 years) had been diagnosed with anxiety and depression, but was careful not to make his pursuit of happiness dependent on gender milestones. "*I try not to allow myself to focus on the belief that I will be happier when… (Insert next stage of medical transition),*" he explained, "*This can* *cause negative thinking that clouds the positive forward movement*". He pointed out that medical transition could be a long process, whilst "*life happens every day*".

For a few participants, it was possible that the original diagnoses they had received pre-transition were not a long-term mental illness, but only related to their gender identity issues. For example, Aid (socially male, 18 years) said that a doctor had tried to diagnose him with depression and anxiety, which Aid instead "*took as symptoms of gender dysphoria*". Four psychologists had subsequently worked with him and said he had no presenting mental illnesses since he had started to express his gender. "*I feel happy and settled now, and very rarely feel upset for long periods of time,*" he said. Some participants had never been formally diagnosed with any mental health issues, such as garfield (male, 31 years) who felt that generally he was "*pretty balanced*". However, factors such as childhood bullying and social exclusion had impacted him, and he did go through a period of very deep depression as a teenager (puberty until late teens), which lifted "*after I started to realise that there was such a thing as transition*". However, for other people, diagnoses such as depression and anxiety remained after transition, arising instead in relation to other catalysts. For Gavin (male/FtM transgender, 23 years), who preferred not to be medicated, his depression was particularly bad before he came out, and he was constantly fatigued and would sleep for days. After seeing a psychologist regularly, and coming out as male to his family and girlfriend, he got better. But sometimes other factors caused him to be depressed such as being overworked, or stress about study. He found when that occurred "*the dysphoria hits me and then I go over the same pattern of my body just shutting down and needing to sleep 24/7 from depression*". Junk000 (male, 22 years) had been diagnosed with anxiety and mood dysregulation (which was possibly chemical), but said that "*neither have to do with my gender identity*". He was frustrated because his doctors "*only ever want to talk about that instead of the problems I want fixed*", slowing his access to gender-related treatments.

Several participants on the discussion board forum openly engaged with topics of mental health diagnoses, telling their stories and making gentle jokes about their own situations. This comic trend may have related to Australian and masculine cultures, and the way Australians tend to make light of serious issues that are awkward to discuss. For example doc79 said "*mental health... yeah I am pretty mental... LOL...*" before telling his story. The discussion board was only intended for a temporary study, but it was clear many of the participants found it useful to have the opportunity to connect online over stressful topics with people who understood their perspectives.

Self-harm

Most of the participants (81 %) had thought about self-harm and for approximately 70 %, their personal issues in regards to their trans* identity were a catalyst. More than half (58 %) referred to other reasons (such as depression or specific incidents

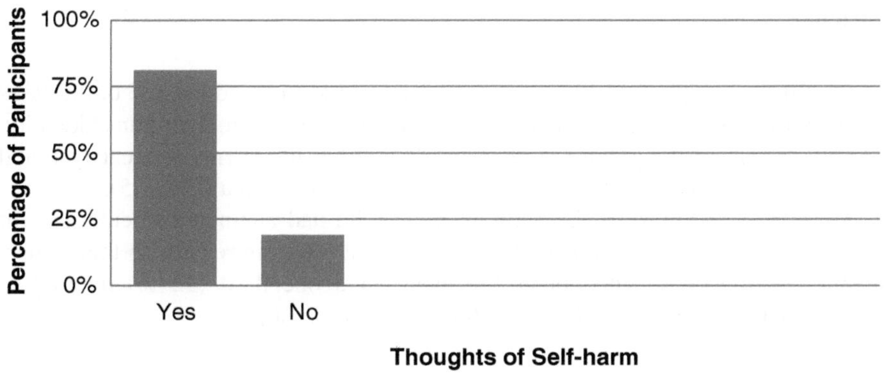

Fig. 7.3 Thoughts of self-harm in *E-male* participants (n = 223)

such as poor surgery outcomes). One third (33 %) cited transphobia as a contributing factor (Fig. 7.3).

A large portion of 68 % of the participants had engaged in self-harm, and this was mostly attributed (70 %) to their personal issues in regards to their trans* identity, followed by other issues in 60 % of the cases, such as body loathing (for example, some respondents reported attempting to 'correct' their chest by attacking it). Finally, a quarter (26 %) referred to experiences of transphobia as a contributing factor. Darkneko (FtM transgender, 21 years) for example reflected that several factors contributed to his self-harm, ranging from depression and social anxiety, to child-hood trauma (Fig. 7.4).

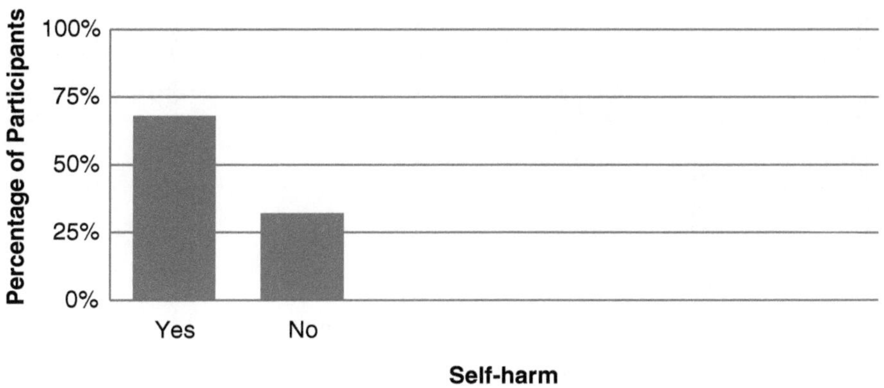

Fig. 7.4 Engagement in self-harm by *E-male* participants (n:220)

Suicide

Most of the group (81 %) had experienced suicidal ideation and in 68 % of the cases these thoughts were linked to their personal issues in regards to their trans* identity. More than half of the group (56 %) referred to other life events as a catalyst, and one third (33 %) related their suicidal ideation to transphobia (Fig. 7.5).

More than one third of the participants (35 %) had attempted suicide and for 76 % these attempts were related to their personal issues in regards to their trans* identity. Half (53 %) cited other life events and one third (32 %) referred to transphobia experiences as a contributing factor (Fig. 7.6).

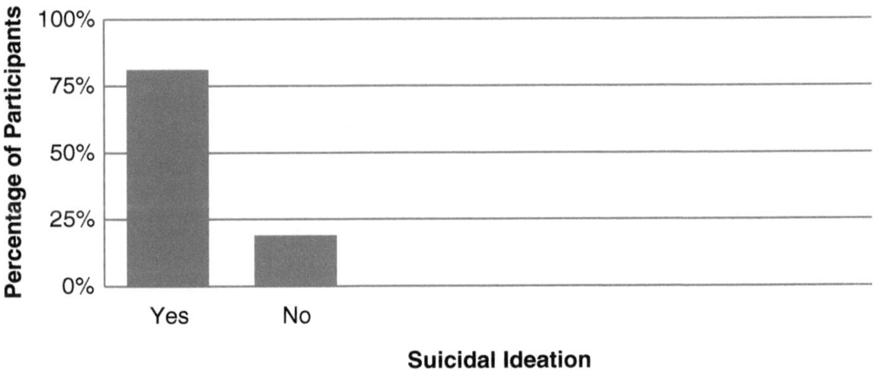

Fig. 7.5 Suicidal ideation rate of *E-male* participants (n = 222)

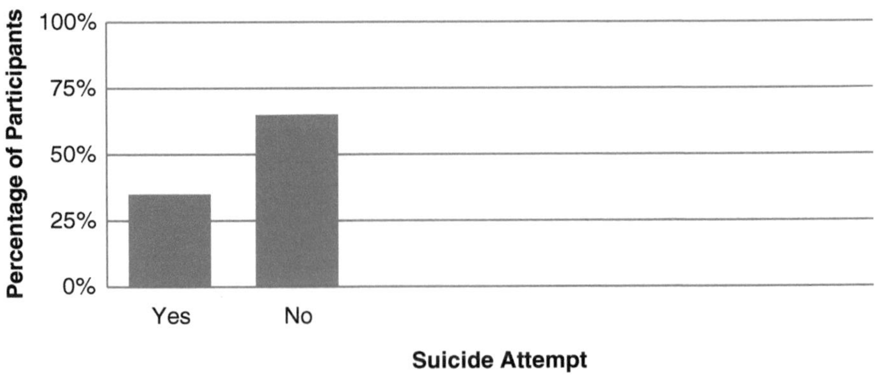

Fig. 7.6 Rate of suicide attempts by *E-male* participants (n:222)

Mental Health Services

We asked about the types of mental health services participants had accessed and why, and their experiences using them. The types of mental health services the participants had used included psychologists, psychiatrists, counselling through sexual health organisations like ACON or mental health organisations like Headspace, gender identity experts, special queer youth counsellors and emergency hotlines like Lifeline. Their motivations for using these services ranged from being "purely for the purposes of paperwork" and diagnosis steps towards starting their transition or specific surgeries, through to dealing with long-term issues in depth. Some sought help in understanding their gender, learning coping skills, or strategizing around how to come out to people and how to best deal with their reactions. There were also specific times of crises, when a participant would seek assistance because they were severely depressed, and in such cases the hotlines were mentioned as the most immediately accessible and helpful service. For many FtM Australians, using mental health services for their gender issues or their mental health needs many times over was not optional, but a necessary requirement for a transition they wished to pursue. This put them in a vulnerable position, as regardless of the quality of services they might need to use them several times over if access to alternatives was limited in their area.

The participants reported mixed experiences in their contact with mental health services. Generally, the services which specialised in gender identity were more useful than the mainstream services. A recurrent topic was the cost of psychiatrist services. Turbogroove (genderqueer, 25 years) had been seeing a psychiatrist for some years, and said "*He hasn't helped me at all and I can barely afford him. He's been condescending for most of the time and doesn't seem to care for the rest of the time*". Other service-providers had offered him contradictory advice. Conor (male, queer, trans*, person of colour, 24 years) found the psychologist and psychiatrist services he sought out in relation to his transition to be variable. *VB* (transsexual male, 32 years) had experienced both a "*brilliant—supportive, informative*" counselling support group run by a trans guy, and a psychiatrist who was "*capitalising on being one of the few who will actually sign off those who want to transition*" and had little knowledge. Whilst he conceded to use the service as "*a stepping stone*", he wished for greater regulation of standards in psychology and psychiatry. *Photoman* (male, 41 years), said that seeing people helped, but found that because there were limited mental health services in his area it took a long time to get to see someone, and when he did "*I only had a few sessions and the psyches then pronounced me cured*". He wanted to feel more time would be put into his issues. Harry (FtM transgender, 24 years) had worked with a psychiatrist who specialised in gender identity, and said "*They have been great. The process has been very simple and they are very knowledgeable and welcoming*". Experienced, affirming gender-focussed providers with streamlined processes, high knowledge and ongoing support were the most valued. Those who focussed specifically on youth issues, coping skills and advice around the social realities of gender diversity were particularly saluted. Expensive and disinterested psychiatrists who did not bulk bill (particularly for required processes that were not optional, and in cases where the patient was known to be in financial difficulty), and service-providers who were unknowledgeable or judgemental, were considered by participants to be the most problematic.

Chapter 8
Education

Abstract Schools can reproduce, or challenge, the restrictive gender norms of society in various ways. This chapter discusses data on education generated by the 273 FtM transgender Australians in the 2013 *E-Males* study. A large portion (69 %) of participants had a post-secondary qualification compared to the general Australian population. Conversely, 4 % had only had a primary school education—twice the portion of the general Australian population. The data suggested that schools were a tougher place for FtM transgender people than post-secondary educational institutions due to the lack of protective school-level policies against transphobia, unisex uniforms and bathrooms, and awareness of transgender issues amongst staff and students—including counsellors. Transphobic discrimination may contribute to some FtM transgender people dropping out of school earlier, whilst transphobic attitudes in the workforce might be keeping FtM people in post-secondary education longer. Some participants had engaged in activisms to somewhat better their circumstances at their schools.

Keywords Transgender · FtM · Visibility · Media · Rights · Law · Research · Theory · Studies · Post-modern

> I don't think any teacher in that school even knew that you could be Trans* and be under the age of 18 (Turbogroove, genderqueer, 25 years).
> I go to an all-girls school, which causes me lots of distress. But I'm at too critical of a point to be able to move schools. I feel it would be hard to be taken seriously as 'a man in a skirt' and that the school would do nothing to help my situation, having not dealt with anything like that before. So it's kind of a 'why bother?' thing. I am 17, not an adult yet. There's a lot of chance that people will say "You're too young to understand what you're talking about." When I'm an adult I'll be more in control and hopefully viewed as someone who is apt at making his own decisions. I plan to come out after graduation, so I'll have been an adult for a while. I also feel that I'm a little unprepared for any questions, so I want to make sure that I can give them a solid understanding of what's going on. I'm overwhelmed by a lot of stuff too right now, school, family, friends, out of school activities… The silence has a huge impact on me daily. I feel a huge weight and pressure from it. I hate being closeted because I can't be who I am. I don't feel that being a transman is anything to hide, but because of those reasons above I don't feel like it's time to come out yet. My family is also under a bit of pressure at the moment and it would be best not to add to that right now. Everyday I'm just catching myself from outing myself. A lot of the time I just want to scream out that

T. Jones et al., *Female-to-Male (FtM) Transgender People's Experiences in Australia*, SpringerBriefs in Sociology, DOI 10.1007/978-3-319-13829-9_8

> "I'm male"! There was a very heated discussion about a transwoman in English which had me trembling from the strength of my emotions. I wonder what they'd say if they knew I'm also transgendered? (Charredmarsh, male, 17 years).

Key Findings

- 69 % of *E-males* participants had a post-secondary qualification—a higher portion than the general Australian population.
- 4 % had not completed secondary school—twice the portion of the general Australian population.
- There was a sense schools could be more problematic than universities in the data.
- Schools largely lacked policies, structural and social supports, and trans* friendly services for transgender students.
- Some participants had cleverly contrived to better their circumstances (in relation to uniform or other themes) within the limited opportunities available to them at school.

Education Level

The data showed a very mixed education context for FtM transgender Australians. On one hand the education level of the *E-males* participants was quite strong—the majority had a post-secondary schooling qualification of some kind (69 %), a higher portion than in the general Australian population (57 %, Australian Bureau of Statistics 2012a). This reflected a similar finding that transgender people were well-educated more broadly from *Tranznation* (Couch et al. 2007). The participants were relatively divided between having post-graduate degrees (19 %) and undergraduate degrees (25 %), TAFE qualifications (25 %), and secondary school certificates (27 %). This high level of post-school study is difficult to explain. One possible explanation is that university networks perhaps contributed to an inflated number of post-graduates participating in the project. However, this seemed unlikely given the data around recruitment sources (which privileged general FtM websites, e-lists and so on). An alternate explanation is the average age of participants (30.5); and their need to be competitive in the contemporary work-force. Another possible explanation is that places of post-school study (universities, TAFEs) might be perceived as "safer" spaces to transition or express one's gender identity than the workforce (which can look into one's gender history indirectly when investigating references

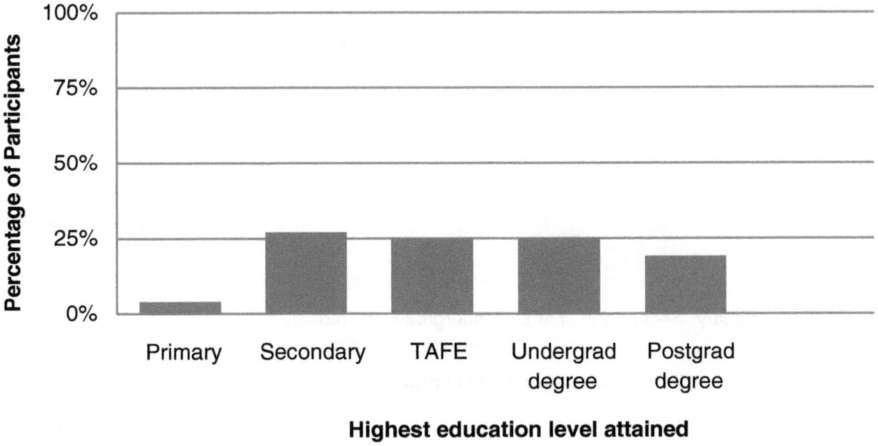

Fig. 8.1 Highest education level completed by *E-males* participants (n = 228)

and so on, and which has had mixed levels of protection for transgender people in the past). It might be the case that *E-males* participants, and FtM transgender Australians more broadly, have been more strongly attracted to educational contexts post-schooling than to generic employment opportunities at certain points in their journey for reasons of safety or support (Fig. 8.1).

On the other hand, a portion of participants had only completed primary school (4 %), and this was twice the portion of the general Australian population who had not attained their high school certificate (2 %, Australian Bureau of Statistics 2012a). This comparison told a very different story to the other statistics on educational attainment. Given that by law Australian young people are required to stay in schools until 15–7 years of age (depending on state and territory laws), this educational disruption suggested that there have been problems for some FtM transgender Australians in school contexts. It seemed most likely that this lower level of school completion reflected the finding in *Writing Themselves in 3* (Hillier et al. 2010; Jones and Hillier 2012) that schools could be problematic for gender questioning young people—who were more likely to have moved schools or dropped out of school as a result of discrimination and bullying than same-sex attracted youth. They were also more likely to have had difficulties at school in concentrating, lower marks and hiding at recess and lunchtime. In addition, young people in *Writing Themselves in 3* had noted that post-school education contexts (universities, TAFE) were often less homophobic and transphobic than secondary schooling contexts, and placed fewer restrictions on one's gender expression generally (around uniforms, gender-based rules and so on) (Fig. 8.2).

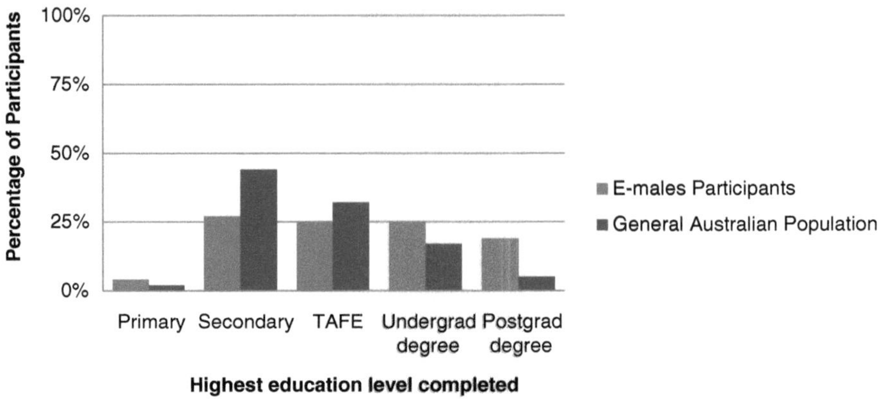

Fig. 8.2 Highest education level completed by *E-males* participants (n = 228), compared to the general Australian population (n = 22,906,400) [As reported by the ABS (2012)]

Policy

In 2013 the SDA Amendment Act (Sexual Orientation, Gender Identity and Intersex Status) made discrimination on the basis of gender identity in the provision of education unlawful. Despite our efforts to have them removed, exemptions for religious schools were supplied in the new law (The Senate Legal and Constitutional Affairs Legislation Committee 2013). This means that religious schools may be able to claim doctrinal exemptions from their obligations to respect students' rights to express their gender identity, although these exceptions to law have not yet been tested. However, as yet the Australian Government has not created a national education policy on transphobia (or homophobia and intersex issues) in schools which could give clearer guidelines on how the law should be enacted. This means that so far, the states and territories have dealt with transgender issues in education policy variably if at all, and in relation to their own state anti-discrimination laws. These state laws also have exemptions for religious schools.

Currently, Victoria's 'Gender identity and students with a transgender or intersex status' policy in the *Victorian Schools Reference Guide* (VIC Government 2007, 4.5.10.11), eight-page document *Supporting Sexual Diversity in Schools* (VIC Government 2008), and HR policy on *Gender Identity* (VIC Government 2009) are the most detailed on transgender student and staff issues. Tasmania's recently added *Guidelines for Supporting Sexual and Gender Diversity in Schools and Colleges* (TAS Department of Education 2012), which was informed in part by a data brief on GLBTIQ students' experiences (Jones 2012a), also stands out. In New South Wales the Teachers Federation issued a policy and kit on *Gender, Sexuality and Identity* (NSW Teachers Federation 2011) to each workplace. South Australia's *Challenging Homophobia in Schools* Guidelines (SA Department for Education and Child Development 2011) include some mention of transgender issues, but are mainly framed around homophobia. It is important to note that Queensland's

Inclusive Education policy is not specific around gender identity (QLD Government 2005),[1] the Australian Capital Territory's anti-bullying and equity policies are more general (ACT Government 2007a, b, c) and the Northern Territory and Western Australia had no relevant policies around transgender students. Western Australia only had policies protecting staff (not students), banning discrimination on the basis of their gender history and orientation (WA Government 2004, p. 7; WA Government Department of Health and Department of Education and Association of Independent Schools WA 2002, p. 4). The Northern Territory had no relevant policies.

The extent to which new generations of transgender students are aware of what protections are and aren't available had not yet been tested, and part of the issue with policy awareness is that students are most likely to be aware of policies only as they pertain to their own personal experience—their particular school (and whether or not a school-level policy reflecting the requirements is developed). The participants were encouraged to comment further on education contexts on the online forum, to deepen our understanding of their experiences of education and policy contexts. They were asked if their school had an anti-bullying policy that protected trans* people. Most of the participants had not experienced roll-out of any of the new policy protections at the school level (if they existed in their state), and the overwhelming majority of respondents answered with a simple "*No*". Some of the group who were over 18 added a brief comment emphasising the point; for example Brett (male/transgender male, 27 years) exclaimed "*Absolutely Not*".

There were a few alternative responses that considered the issue in relation to a general lack of attention to bullying more broadly. For example, Draconem (FtM transgender, 24 years) said "*They didn't really have an anti-bullying policy for anyone*", and Garfield (male, 31 years) said "*high school: no—general bullying policy, not well enforced, no trans specific stuff*". However, one encouraging experience was reported by Harry (FtM transgender, 24 years); his answer emphasised the possibility that schools and universities could be supportive spaces for some FTM Australians: "*There is always some kind of anti-bullying policy. At high school, I'm unsure exactly what was in place. At uni there is definitely a policy that protects trans people*".

Information Provision

Proposed national curricula inclusion of GLBTIQ issues in sex education and health had been deleted from the most recent draft of the forthcoming *Australian National Curriculum* at time of print, to the outcry of many advocates and

[1] Although the researchers acknowledge that efforts have been made to reframe the QLD policy to now apply to issues such as homophobia, which was a step forward in 2013: http://education.qld.gov.au/actsmartbesafe/schoolleaders/racism-homophobia.html.

researchers—including ourselves (McNeilage 2013). We had previously found coverage of gender non-conformity and transgender issues in schools in the field of sex education to be minimal (Jones 2011a, b; Jones and Hillier 2012, 2013). The *E-males* participants were asked if their school provided any information to students about trans* identities or issues more broadly (in sex education, science or any other subject). The majority of respondents again simply answered "*No*". A few expanded on this; for example Darkneko (FtM transgender, 21 years) said:

> No school taught us about LGBT things. It was a very hush hush kind of thing. No information was made available even discreetly in the form of pamphlets and library books. The school system just pretends that everyone is straight.

Harry (FtM transgender 24 years) commented on the greater information provision at his university; "*Nope, never. I'm sure there's some kind of gender studies class at uni though. Other than that there is nothing*".

Counselling

The respondents were asked if their school provided a trans* friendly counsellor. The responses were mostly definite "nos" (particularly from those with experience in dealing with the counsellors), but there was also much uncertainty (particularly from those who did not got to the counsellor). Eric (FtM transgender, age 49 years) emphasised that such a counsellor was unthinkable in his school days; "*I left school 30 years ago and at the time there were no services of the kind you describe. No awareness either*". Junk000, (male, 22 years) who attended an all-girls private school in the 2000s, responded in the doubting manner typical of those who were unsure; "*Don't know, suspect not*". There was a strong message that many of the counsellors were indeed unsupportive of, or untrained in, trans* issues. It was additionally clear that even if counsellors were in principal supportive, in practice they were not communicating this to their students (or our participants) through their general messages or office features (such as posters/stickers on the door indicating a trans* friendly space). Only one participant was absolutely certain of having a school counsellor who was supportive of their identity.

Uniforms

We asked the participants if their school had unisex uniform options (outfits someone of any sex/gender identity could wear). No participant attended a school where a specifically unisex or gender neutral uniform was standard. Some emphasised that they instead attended single sex schools in their youth where feminine styles such as dresses, skirts and stockings were mandatory. Even in contexts where PE uniforms were unisex or "neutral", respondents mainly specified that these clothes were reserved only for sports. There were sometimes punishments meted out to those who tried to wear their sports shorts, pants and jerseys outside the context of sport; Gavin (male/FtM transgender, 23 years) for example noted, "*Lunch time detention was awarded to those who broke the rule consistently... Catholic girls' school*".

Some participants however did attend schools where, whilst there were not unisex options as such, there were a range of options for girls which they benefited from greatly. For example, Darkneko said, "*No unisex options were available, but girls were allowed to wear long pants and shorts instead of skirts*". There were also contexts which had been markedly improved by the clever manoeuvrings of *E-males* participants themselves. Brett (male/transgender male, 27 years) recounted how he deftly machinated some advocacy towards a greater range in girls' uniforms, not as a trans issue but as a women's issue, making use of the structures available to him at the time to support his needs: "*As part of the student committee I got trousers in for girls in high school. Although I was the only one wearing it. Fuck dresses*".

Bathrooms

The media has made much of cases wherein transgender kids wished to use bathrooms congruent with their gender identity at school, and in one case this extra attention famously helped a Queensland school to at last become more supportive of the student's need (Dibben 2013). Given the likelihood that this ground-breaking case had not yet become standard, we instead investigated if there had at least been some unisex bathroom options (toilets someone of any sex/gender identity could use) at the schools our participants attended. The respondents all answered "no", in relation to both the schools and post-schooling education institutions they had attended. Some participants mentioned occasionally seeking to use the staff toilets on the days when they were permitted, but this was a rarity. In addition, Maddox (male/ftm/transman, 21 years) noted "*We had two sets of disabled toilets, but they weren't accessible to able-bodied students*". Maddox's distinction about able-bodied students is important to remember in light of the fact that most of the *E-males* participants *did not* identify as disabled, and are not classified as such. In the researchers' experience some schools have sought to let transgender students use the disabled toilets as a kind of temporary solution during transition periods for example. But we believe this is not useful long-term for someone who does not identify as having a disability and is recognisably able-bodied in the minds of other students, compared to having a unisex bathroom anyone can access without the need to declare any particular identity, or allowing students to use the bathroom congruent with their gender identity.

Attitudes

Schools were not seen as trans-positive environments. Several participants commented that their single sex schools offered no other option than to act like the intake gender, or that there was a sense that alternatives simply did not exist. Doc79 (male, 33 years) remarked on the impact of gender norms on attitudes towards FtM transgender people at his co-ed school; "*Girls were girls and boys were boys... if you didn't act that way it was assumed that you must be gay (butch or fairy were the terms usually used)*". Aid (socially male, 18 years) summed up the general attitude to his gender identity at school as, "*Not accepted. You had to stick to strict gender norms or teachers involved your parents*". Brett (male/transgender male, 27 years) said, "*My Primary and high school had an extremely bad attitude towards Trans. It was a strict Catholic school. It was horrible. Many bad things happened to me in that school*". This reflected other findings about the prevalence of homophobic and transphobic attitudes at many schools (Hillier et al. 2010).

Being Yourself at School

Previous reports by doctors of Australian Transgender MtF students suggested that the individuals they spoke to were under great pressure not be themselves at school (McCredie 2008), and we were keen to see the extent to which FtM students were under such pressure. Unfortunately, participants largely commented that it was simply not possible to be themselves or express their identity with the school's direct support. Those who attended an all-girls school were given no real workable options to express themselves. For example Garfield said he was "*discouraged from doing anything 'unladylike'*". But there were even difficulties in other school contexts. Turbogroove (genderqueer, 25 years) emphasised that attempts to be himself were "*Strongly Discouraged*". Maddox said, "*I had no other uniform option but a dress, I would have been bullied so I didn't ever talk to anyone about anything close to myself*". Aid said that the school responded to efforts to be himself by forcing him to "*wear skirts and small tight shirts*", adding "*Short hair was frowned upon and I was forced to see a counsellor*". Junk000 said he simply wasn't taught that FTM Trangender identities existed. Harry said, "*High school—no. I came out as gay and that didn't go down well at all. Uni—there is a LGBTI group but I've never seen them have any presence around the uni*". Doc79 said it was "not really" possible; "*I was kind of labelled a little butch*". However, there was a sense that it was sometimes possible to for an FtM transgender person to orchestrate some opportunities for expression without the *direct support* of the school—Darkneko explained, "*As an FtM it was possible as I could just wear long pants and shorts instead of skirts, and have short hair or dress like a boy on mufti days. But an MtF transgender person would have not been tolerated*".

Ideas for Improvement

We asked what the *E-males* participants felt would have improved their experience in the school system. Most respondents reported that they wanted to see more education and information provision on transgender concepts—that it exists, what it can mean, that it's an affirmed and protected set of characteristics in law and part of broader GLBTIQ diversity. They felt that whether this was learned in general classes, special courses, sex education, the rules or the library resources was less important than ensuring it was not simply only discussed "in the playground" (which was seen as a potentially cruel space and often a source of misinformation). For example, Doc79 said, "*If they can teach that some kids have two mums, or two dads, then surely they can teach that not everyone who was born one sex will remain that sex...*".

Unisex options for the school uniform were another key theme. Gavin remarked, "*Let me wear the sports uniform, I looked awkward enough in their frilly dress*!" Other features such as supportive school counsellors and other topics explored above were mentioned; Maddox particularly wanted to see all the support features discussed in the project (from information provision to unisex bathrooms). He added, "*the education system I experienced did not mention gender or sexuality differences. That is a shame and it should be changed. These educational changes will save lives*". Turbogroove and others pointed to the need for teacher education; "*Maybe add some type of education about LGBTs to the course people have to take to become teachers? Maybe a compulsory seminar?*". Garfield underlined the importance of supportiveness from a teacher; "*I had a couple of teachers who were very supportive of me as an unhappy and conflicted individual. Everyone needs that*". Other ideas included stricter, clearer rules against transphobia and homophobia; more inclusive sex education; queer spaces.

Chapter 9
Employment

Abstract This chapter examines data on employment generated by the 273 FtM transgender Australians in the 2013 *E-Males* study. The majority of participants (58 %) were working (full-time, part-time or in an apprenticeship). However, 15 % were unemployed—a higher portion than in previous studies on broader populations. The qualitative data revealed there were clear obstacles to employment and promotion for FtM transgender people. These included the fear of coming out as transgender, transphobia both in recruitment and on-site, the desire to avoid work during transition, and uncertainty around the need to reveal gender history in applications. Some workplaces and industries were perceived as more supportive than others, and there were examples of sites with very transphobic masculine work cultures that had compromising impacts even on men who had fully transitioned and "passed" as male. Leadership had a pivotal role in whether workplaces were transphobic or supportive; poor and best-practice examples are described.

Keywords Transgender · FtM · Employment · Work · Job · Industry · Rights · History · Leadership · Legal

> My voice has always been a problem in jobs. I just get weird looks, but that's about it. When I first started working in an all-male environment in a warehouse, I did get some problems. I wasn't used to the kind of antics that happen, or the pranks. I had my supervisor say I was a big girl, and he pretended to push my head down and told me to suck his cock. When I reported it, I was told that if I couldn't handle a male environment I could be "moved"... So I made up some lame excuse about being stressed because of family problems and took a few days leave. I returned to work with a stronger front; I joined in with some of the jokes and pranks (as long as they didn't hurt anyone or were not offensive or racist etc.). So I started to fit in a little more, and I got more responsibility in the workforce. I had one guy joke around with me that I was probably a guy with a fanny who had testosterone injections to grow a beard. That made me feel a little nervous as I thought he knew something I didn't want him to. But when I made a joke about him being a twat himself everyone laughed, and nothing was said again (doc79, male, 33 years).

> I've worked for the same organization for over 2 years and been transitioning for just over one year. They've been very supportive. I asked my Supervisor to speak to my colleagues and Head Office for me and within a few days the majority of staff were calling me by my

T. Jones et al., *Female-to-Male (FtM) Transgender People's Experiences in Australia*, SpringerBriefs in Sociology, DOI 10.1007/978-3-319-13829-9_9

> preferred name as if nothing had happened. They were very supportive when I took time off for chest surgery and I was able to return on light duties without issue (Batman, other/transitioning, 27 years).

Key Findings

- The majority of participants (58 %) were working (full-time, part-time or in an apprenticeship).
- 15 % were unemployed.
- Obstacles to employment and promotion included fear of coming out as transgender, transphobia, the desire to avoid work during transition, uncertainty around the need to reveal gender history in a job or police check applications, and fear of exposure in certain environments.
- Some workplaces and industries were perceived as more supportive than others.
- Leadership (supervisors, management and so on) had a pivotal role in whether workplaces were transphobic or supportive.

Employment Status

Whilst around a third of the *E-males* participants were engaged in study, the majority were employed (58 %): full-time (34 %), part-time (22 %), or in an apprenticeship (2 %). However, a sizeable portion of the participants were unemployed (15 %)—a difference in comparison to the general Australian population that is perhaps made more poignant by the fact that this was a highly educated group, with an average age of 30.5 (an age level associated with greater employment stability in Australian culture). The rate of unemployment was higher than the 9 % for the general transgender population cited in *Tranznation* (Couch et al. 2007) and the 9 % for FtM transgender people cited in *Private Lives* (Pitts et al. 2006).

Income

The *E-males* participants had a range of annual incomes. At first glance the income earned by the group seems relatively low, with the majority (52 %) under $41K per year. Moreover, 43 % were earning less than $20K, and this is a significantly larger portion than the 35 % in *Tranznation* (Couch et al. 2007) and the 22 % in *Private Lives* (Pitts et al. 2006). Perhaps this could be partially explained by the fact that a third of the respondents were engaged in study, 24 % had a reduced earning capacity due to working part-time or within an apprenticeship, and 15 % were

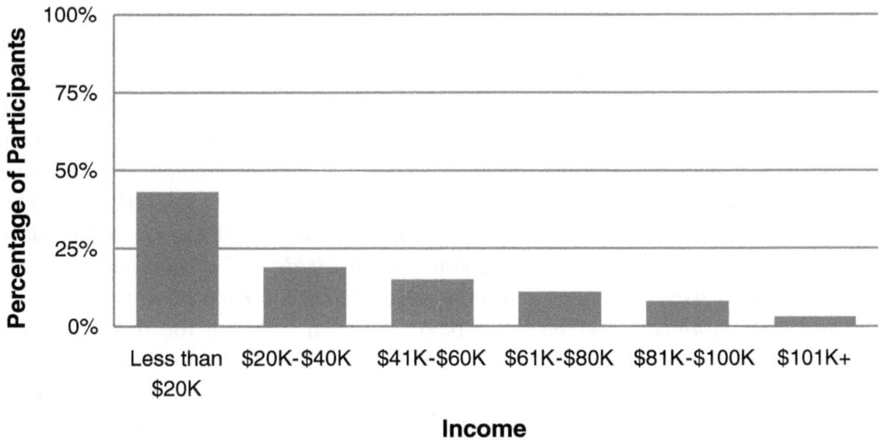

Fig. 9.1 Income of *E-males* participants (n = 227)

unemployed. There were also participants earning a range of salaries: 15 % earned $41K–$60K, 11 % earned $61K–$80K, and 8 % earned $81K–$100K, 3 % earned over $100K. So whilst a smaller portion of the participants were earning the higher wages than across Australian populations more broadly, and they seemed to be earning less than expected for such a well-educated group, the data showed it was certainly achievable for this population to be gainfully employed. The research team surmised that while other factors (such as study, other priorities or perhaps particular issues in gaining work) might be impacting the group's income, the fact that transgender people have repeatedly been seen to earn less than the general Australian population in other studies confirmed that there are likely issues related to transgender status impacting employment, pay rates and promotions for this group (Fig. 9.1).

Employment Obstacles

To further understand the distinct nature of the issues that arose for FtM transgender people around unemployment and lower incomes according to the quantitative survey data, we invited the *E-males* participants on the forum to discuss whether their gender identity had ever become an obstacle for their career or employment aspirations. This investigation uncovered a range of issues that varied depending on whether the participant was not "out" but being read as their allocated birth sex by colleagues, was in the process of some kind of transition, or had transitioned and was being read as "male" (and not transgender).

For the group who were not "out" (but generally being read as their allocated birth sex by colleagues) there were concerns about losing their job if they were to disclose their gender identity or consider transitioning further. Junk000 (a younger male who does not yet "pass") is not out at his current job. He has been applying for jobs outside of it but the employers "*keep fretting about 'but which bathroom will you use?' and how I am 'a HR nightmare'; ridiculous things like that*". He fears he will lose his current job or miss out on job opportunities if he comes out, and worse that he won't even be informed about it; "*I'm sure they're vaguely aware that's against some law somewhere. They will still do it, they just won't tell me*". Fang (FtM transgender, 29 years) had similar fears, and said that at his job he had only disclosed his trans* status to one person; "*I am afraid if I disclose it I will be excluded until I leave, yet I am also concerned that when I am passing as male it will not go unnoticed*". Yet he hates being called a "she" in the meantime. He described this Catch-22 as "*a constant source of anxiety in the workplace*". Many people in this group felt like there was no escape from the stress at work. But they were unlikely to invest in "coming out" if they wouldn't be at the job for a long period. Maddox (male/ftm/transman, 21 years) was an example of a participant who chose not to come out at such a job pre-transition, but only to come out to colleagues after having left such a role and later on in his journey.

For the second group of participants (who were in the process of transitioning in some way), it was not uncommon to avoid work altogether. Within this group, some said they engaged in study during the period of transition to delay their need to become employed and declare a more stable identity. But even for those engaged in study and internships towards their chosen career, there could be problems; Kafka said that when studying law he still faced difficulties, mainly around "all the questioning". A few did look for work at times, but cited a sense of confusion about how to apply for work given their conflicting gender identity, presentation and/or history; or non-conforming expression. For example, Draconem (FtM transgender, 24 years) said, "*I feel like it's only made it hard for me to figure out how to apply for work*". Several participants reported confusion over how to apply for police checks. They were unsure whether they were to tick "m" or "f" on the form about their history, and whether that would out them to potential employers in fields where police checks were mandatory (care, education and so on). Others particularly did not want to have to work "as a female", and had waited for (and were waiting for) particular transition milestones to pass before engaging in employment. For example, Harry said;

> Besides the depression and anxiety, which kept me unemployed, I didn't want to have to out myself at work or have to work as a female. So I waited until I was passing consistently enough not to have to worry. Luckily this only took three months on T.

For the third group of participants who had either already transitioned, been read as "male" socially or were otherwise living their life in a way congruent with their gender identity, there were many who had not discussed their gender identity at work at all. In some cases they found this prevented many issues. However, commencing work as a male could present problems for some. Garfield (male, 31 years) recounted how he had intended to be socially transitioned before starting his first job, in order to avoid being seen as female or transgender. Unfortunately, while he managed to get the right name on his degree, he was still presenting as female when he started his first job, so he did not come out regarding his transition process. That led to "*some interesting moments*" when being interviewed for his second job as a male, particularly in terms of reference checking. He explained, "*I think the boss at the new job just convinced himself he misheard the pronouns on the phone to my old boss when he was doing the reference checking*". However, the second job involved a lot of travel in the outback with other male staff members. This often involved camping in areas where toilet facilities were often non-existent. "*I didn't have a useable 'stand to pee' device. I spent most of that job absolutely terrified of discovery*". This meant that he changed career directions to avoid his gender history becoming revealed, despite really enjoying the work.

Particular environments were also more problematic than others for a transitioned male. For example, Doc79 recounted the pressure to put up with or even conform to workplace cultures of engaging in transphobic banter and abusive pranks in all-male warehouse environments, because he was perceived as a male and not a transgender person. There were times when his supervisor called him a "big girl" and engaged in acts which constituted sexual harassment—that were later brushed off as something he should be able to "handle". He noticed that joining in jokes and pranks actually benefitted his career, even to the extent of taking and "giving back" relatively transphobic language. This negatively impacted his confidence around his identity, and illustrated the need for all workplaces—even those that seem not to have transgender employees—to engage in equity training in line with the updated legal protections around gender identity (for staff, supervisors and management). It showed, along with the other examples, that employers cannot make assumptions about the gender identity or history of their staff. Further, employers cannot make assumptions about the ways in which transphobic cultures might be impacting any of their staff members; who may be trans* but not out, may have transitions in their gender history, and/or may have loved ones who are trans*.

Employment Supports

The 2013 SDA Amendment Act (Sexual Orientation, Gender Identity and Intersex Status) made discrimination on the basis of gender identity in employment unlawful, with some exemptions for religious organisations. There are also some state level employment protections. However, there is a way to go clearly before these have a stronger impact, given some of the recent negative experiences discussed by participants. In addition, there were people who felt vulnerable even with protections in place due to the nature of their casual or contract employment basis, such as Fang (FtM transgender, 29 years), who said, "*I know there are new guidelines but I have trouble seeing how this protects me at the moment, being in casual employment*". Ramir (transgender, 25 years) commented on the fact that there is greater support available in creative and care-based industries, compared some of the more conservative or gender conforming industries:

> I feel extremely lucky to work in a few different places, where the people I work with appreciate me for the person that I am, not my gender. I know this isn't the case for most trans* people. Some of this is the fact that I work in the creative arts and disabilities, so there is alot more understanding and embracing of difference in all it's forms.

Xzaclee (male, 35 years) took advantage of working in a medical environment with particular supports. There were also participants who engaged in self-employment or were on benefits as a means of creating supportive contexts for themselves for a time. But really the spirit of non-discrimination supports should include a vision for FtM transgender Australians (and others) to be able to engage in all types of employment and any industries they wish to engage in (or in which their skills-base falls), rather than being restricted to "safer" or "more accepting" options.

In contexts where participants had enjoyed supportive environments, there was also often a sense that this was a "one-off"—a trait of a particular business or group of people. For example, Darkneko commented that at his old job, employers and staff "were fine with" his gender identity and transition. But he was concerned about getting employment again; "*I know I will have to be a male at work too. I couldn't stop even if I wanted to*". Batman (other/transitioning, 27 years) reflected that the organisation he had worked at for over two years had been "very supportive" of his transition, which had been ongoing over the past year. He asked his supervisor to speak to his colleagues and Head Office for him about the matter, and reported that "*within a few days the majority of staff were calling me by my preferred name as if nothing had happened*". They were very supportive when he took time off for chest surgery and he was able to return on light duties without issue. This example showed how clear support from management and supervisors, combined with clear guidelines for the employee's colleagues, can enable FtM Australians to experience the kind of workplace environment that they all have every right to enjoy. It was overall very clear from the participants' stories that leadership on this issue could make a big difference in the employees' experiences and the workplace culture around gender identity, for better or worse.

Chapter 10
Discrimination, Social Acceptance and Support

Abstract Discrimination against transgender people on the basis of their gender identity or expression is illegal in Australia, however it is not always easy for Australian transgender people to find adequate social support. This chapter examines data on discrimination and social support generated by the 273 FtM transgender Australians in the 2013 *E-Males* study. Some participants had no experiences of discrimination on the basis of transphobia, others had experienced public humiliation and verbal and/or physical abuse. Coming out was fraught with difficulties including the potential end of key relationships. Mostly, it was a positive experience in that it relieved self-doubt, generated understanding and supported transitions. Sometimes participants felt they had to be advocates for FtM transgender communities, other times they reported "going stealth" for safety reasons or to more fully embody their gender identity. Respondents' general wellbeing and quality of life was significantly influenced by relationships with family, friends and intimate partners.

Keywords Transgender · FtM · Discrimination · Transphobia · Abuse · Harassment · Social · Support · Family · Friend

> I have copped physical and verbal abuse a dozen times over my gender identity. Mostly from cisgender guys bullying me to physically prove my "manhood", because in their mind I am lacking in masculinity. Most rude or discriminatory comments I believe simply come from ignorant people who do not understand, or misunderstand, what it means to identify as transgender (Maddox, male/ftm/transman, 21 years).

> This email from my girlfriend's mum is beautiful. I showed it to some of my trans brothers and we were all in tears! She said: 'It takes a lot of guts to be unique with integrity, but I can see how both you and [my girlfriend] are beautiful examples of young people daring to live a unique life with integrity. I find that inspiring. I think it is exactly what Jesus was trying to show us as well, but what a lot of people don't seem to get. It got him killed in the end, but till the very last moment he could lovingly forgive the people that did not get him and hated him. What carried him through was knowing that He was deeply loved by God himself. We will pray every day that you will know that as well, that the real you is uniquely created and deeply loved. Not only by God, also by us!' I am very grateful for her love and support, and how 100 % confident she is talking about it too, with other family members etc. She has told a lot of that side of the family. She is going to have coffee with my mum when I do tell my parents, and I'm sure it will be really helpful (Ramir, transgender, 25 years).

T. Jones et al., *Female-to-Male (FtM) Transgender People's Experiences in Australia*, SpringerBriefs in Sociology, DOI 10.1007/978-3-319-13829-9_10

Key Findings

- Some people had experienced no discrimination on the basis of transphobia, others had experienced public humiliation and verbal and/or physical abuse.
- Coming out was fraught with difficulties, including the weight of keeping a secret and the potential end of key relationships. Mostly, coming out was a positive experience in that it relieved self-doubt, helped others better understand trans-identity and supported transitions.
- Respondents' general wellbeing and quality of life was significantly influenced by relationships with family, friends and intimate partners.
- Difficulties in key relationships created distrust of others, support from these relationships seemed to increase general happiness.
- Positive social experiences were the result of accepting and non-judgemental family members, friends, queer peers, health professionals, colleagues and institutions.

Discrimination

Some of the participants had never experienced discrimination. However, they acknowledged that this was a possibility they were always aware of (such as Draconem, FtM transgender, 24 years). Others had experienced being called names like 'freak', 'faggot' and 'dyke' on the street or at school; including for example photoman (male, 41 years), who said "*I have had a few people abuse me, calling me a freak and the like. Some of my acquaintances do not accept me as male*". There were also accounts of public shaming by church communities. For example, one participant aged in his thirties, who had been with his church community for some years, was removed from his position within the religious organisation on the basis of his gender history. He also had his gender identity discussed and debated by the organisation with other members in his absence and in his presence, without his permission.

There were instances where people were verbally or physically abused by cisgender men in groups, who were trying to get them to prove their masculinity—including Maddox (male/ftm/transman, 21 years), who described this happening around a dozen times. In other cases the group assault was apparently on the basis of homophobia, because the participant was assumed to be gay or lesbian by the assailants:

> I have been physically abused in the street for appearing to be a "faggot" and verbally abused for appearing to be a "dyke". I do not defend my gender identity to strangers, though, so it's not known to them (Junk000, male, 22 years).

Others described being chased by thugs wielding bottles and rocks:

> While I was transitioning, and in a period when I looked ambiguous gender-wise, I was chased down the street by a small gang of thugs wielding bottles and rocks. That was unpleasant and scary (Garfield, male, 31 years).

Participants' comments suggested that aggressors particularly targeted people who were gender non-conforming or in the process of transition for street violence. This suggested a strong need for social inclusion campaigns around people who look different.

Following their experience of abuse and discrimination, some respondents indicated that they were no longer trustful of others. Others experienced doubts about their self-worth and social acceptability. For example, photoman admitted that he no longer trusted many people, and found it "*hard to be around people at times.*" In addition, the man who had been shamed by his church reflected:

> Six months ago I had the beginning of a large Christian family; friends who I would socialise with, study with and who cared about me. I cared about them. Now I am back to thinking I shouldn't bother trying to be close to people again.

Maddox said:

> Copping physical and verbal abuse has lowered my self-esteem and self-confidence. This kind of treatment has made me embarrassed and ashamed of who I am. It also has made me anxious and fearful of social changes and situations like meeting new people, going out to social public places like clubs and bars, and new changes (like a change in Uni or work).

Junk000 commented:

> I suspect now that people will punch me on the street more for being queer. I'm probably more at risk of physical abuse than when I just presented as a drab female.

Garfield had stopped being forthcoming about his identity, and like many feared social and physical consequences in a range of environments. "*I suspect it would be a problem for me if people I work with knew about it,*" he supposed, "*but luckily they don't*".

Coming Out

Being comfortable with one's gender identity is an integral factor in feeling ready to indicate to one's transformation to others. However, readiness to 'come out' about an identity can be fraught with concerns and realities about being ostracised and excluded from hard-won social support networks including friendships, family and institutions (as seen above). For some, this resulted in selectively sharing their gender identity with a small number of people, allowing others to control their coming out process, waiting to share their identity until a later date or simply not sharing that side of their lives at all. Draconem (FtM transgender, 24 years) had not had any negative feedback from friends, but his family was "*still coming to terms with it...*"; particularly his mother. Several members of his immediate family were struggling to use his preferred pronouns. He did not want to hide it from other people in his extended family who had known him growing up, but his mum said "*I shouldn't tell my family just yet*". Zane, (male, 21 years) had told his parents, "*who did not accept it at first, but have later come to accept it*". Zane also told his (now) ex-girlfriend who "*completely withdrew her support*". His parents had informed various family members who had dealt well with the change. Zane said "*I'm not comfortable with all my family and their friends knowing, but I know there is no other way*". After his negative experiences, he explained, "*I would never tell people I personally know*", and instead relied on his parents to manage his coming out process.

Charredmarsh (male, 17 years) had a strong desire to be open about his gender identity, but felt he could not come out fully to any of his family yet. His mother had found about it when he was under a lot of pressure, but they didn't discuss it and "*it wasn't taken seriously*". He was afraid of upsetting his family, whom he lived with and relied on financially. Not coming out fully had made his relationships with people quite tense. It made him act in antisocial ways, because he could not handle being constantly seen as female. He also felt hurt by remaining in the closet about something he was proud about. He had come out to around six of his 20 friends however. "*I needed to open up to someone, to get a bit of the weight off of my shoulders but also to seek support and find out what someone would think,*" he explained. "*The pressure of being not open is far too much for me*". The friends gave mixed responses:

> I have a (now) very close friend who I disclosed my gender identity to. The way she responded blew my mind really. This close friend is very supportive, she is open about talking about it and treats me like who I am. Her first question was 'Do you want me to use male pronouns?' and I hadn't yet had the courage to ask anyone. She's really caring and knows just what to say and do really. Another friend I'd told (my girlfriend at the time) sort of left it unsaid after that. I didn't bring it up much either because she didn't seem interested. The other friends brushed it off and a lot of them seem to have forgotten about it now. They use my male name as a 'nickname', but still use female pronouns. Except for two who occasionally correct themselves. Another friend I came out to exclaimed 'What?!" loudly and doesn't quite seem to get it. She was mostly shocked but did nothing and hasn't mentioned it since. Since I'm not really out no one has changed their treatment of me (Charredmarsh, male, 17 years).

There were people in the study who were in the process of coming out, but were finding it difficult due to the fact they had children. Eli (transitioning, 29 years), had been absorbed in raising a three year old son and "*put it off for that reason*", citing the pressure and the stigma of being a "good mum" as a major barrier to coming out. However, he decided that he deserved to be happy and "*true to myself*". Whilst still having doubts about starting hormones, "*mainly for the unknown future of my relationship with my son*", he was proceeding regardless. Disclosure to adult family members and friends had mainly been a positive experience and had "*made it seem more real*". However, the main question he received was "*have you thought about how it could be for your son?*" Eli argued that the impact of silence had "*really just led me to being unhappy, and trying to 'fix' everything else not related to being transgender*". He was about to start testosterone and see how that impacted his relationships.

Several participants resented the idea that they had to "come out". Some felt it put them in a dangerous position. Another participant said, "*I already came out as lesbian many years ago, and that was one of the roughest times of my life*". He feared family rejection again. He added:

> It pisses me off that my brothers don't have to "come out" as cis-gendered or straight. I'm not at all secretive, I'm a very honest and open person. But I wish I didn't have to sit down with everyone important (or not even) and tell them personally about my identity. Why can't I just be who I am? It bothers me that people feel betrayed if I don't personally tell them. I would like to just live my life as the person I am, and talk to people when it comes up, not having to feel the pressure of not putting something on Facebook etc. because I haven't had the chance to sit down with everyone I know! I'm just so sick of the pressure of all these labels flying around. If I could have been the person I am, freely, for my whole life, I wouldn't have to do any 'coming out', because I would have always been free to be me, whatever form that took in the particular moment.

However, having to wait to come out sometimes exacerbated negative thoughts about oneself or the ability to 'pass' as a man. This was sometimes the result of fear of the social exclusion, judgement and scrutiny which some of the transmen experienced once they disclosed their gender identity. Gavin (male/FtM transgender, 23 years) said:

> It is hard at times; especially if I get depressed (not often). But if I do, I crash. When I hadn't come out to anyone I was diagnosed with depression and anxiety for about three years and had constant fatigue. I was just out of high school and in my first year of university at college and I had to move back home because of my depression. I finally saw someone about it. I deferred my studies to focus on myself. Mum and dad didn't believe me and said I hadn't met the right man. My doctor said 'You are a beautiful girl, you are just a lesbian. There is no need to mutilate your body with surgery and testosterone'.

Although respondents may have felt reluctant to discuss their gender identity with certain people it seemed that those who had gone through the process of coming out and facing negative feedback indicated that "it gets better". Several people discussed how disclosure made their life difficult for a time, but over the longer term things improved and parents became more supportive (sometimes after eight years or more). Nikozilar (male, 20 years) was another example of someone who came out to his parents many years before they accepted it. He was 14 when he first told them, and they were only just starting to come around after six years. However, there were people who had permanently lost friends, or who had experienced progress to a certain point with loved ones, but then temporary regressions of support with various milestones. For example, thewaywesee (trans* male or queer male, 22 years) said his father was initially supportive but "*became less supportive when I legally changed my name*" because this milestone had made the transition suddenly seem more serious for him. He was only slowly becoming more open-minded to his son again.

Many people described coming out as being "a weight off their shoulders". It was rarely a singular process but involved many "coming outs" over time, which often made the process easier and gave them a chance to refine their different methods. Some indicated that being open about their identity was necessary to promote their wellbeing and to successfully engage in healthy (intimate) relationships. One participant reflected that for him, "*emotional, physical, and mental intimacy feels impossible without someone having my full context*", and he had decided that if he wanted to be intimate with someone, he would disclose first. Others also explained that disclosing had deepened their intimacy with people and strengthened their trust in the relationship or friendship.

Being an Advocate

Although it was difficult, some transmen took it upon themselves to act as educational or social advocates about trans-identity. This may have been in response to the denial that the transmen experienced from family, friends, colleagues or health professionals about trans-identity. *Bearcooking* (male, 58 years) had been living full time as a male for quite a number of years, but discussed his gender history with people he knew were "*open to difference*" in order to educate them. He reflected: "*Being open is a plus, and helps people to understand differences and similarities, taking the mysticism out of the 'Hollywood version'*". Jay (male, 30 years) commented that he was "*more than happy*" to educate people on trans issues and who he was, but only if they were open and willing to listen. Others felt that in coming out and discussing other GLBTIQ issues freely, they added to the many voices that were helping young people in the future to have an easier experience. There were some who limited their advocacy to GLBTIQ or trans* contexts only, and used it purely to help young trans* people or their allies in safe spaces, to give tips or insights. GLBTIQ spaces were used by many as a place to overcome, and help others overcome, the personal issues with being transgender that so many people cited as having a negative impact on well-being.

Darkneko (FtM transgender, 21 years) had experienced violent reactions from family when he first came out. But said he was nevertheless open to other people about being transgender for many reasons:

> One reason is I feel the need to be open about it. I can't keep it a secret without destroying myself. Another is I think it gives strength and courage to other transgender people to see someone out and proud. I'm not saying that I want to be a hero or icon. But for me, knowing others were like me made all the difference. I felt less freaky. I disclosed to my work mates who were aged in their teens and twenties. At first they were confused and assumed a lot of untrue things. I know it wasn't their fault when they said some not nice stuff or laughed, because they did not understand. I invited them to ask questions and learn more. I like to think I made a difference, but who knows? They seemed more curious than harmful really. I answered dozens of questions about being trans. And yes, some of those questions could be considered stupid or hurtful. But they did learn.

He felt he had found out who his real friends were through being transparent. Whilst the negative responses had certainly affected him, the positive impact he was making made it all worthwhile. Some respondents felt very comfortable being transgender FtM, and even wanted to incorporate this comfort into an advocacy-based career.

Going Stealth

Coming out was not an ideal shared by everyone in the study. Some people preferred privacy and felt that their gender history, or gender identity, was not public property. Several people spoke of the concept of "stealth": either passing as a man without aids, transitioning fully and not telling anyone about their gender history, or presenting as a masculine female/gender fluid person without specific explanation or coming out processes. They used phrases like "*need to know basis*", "*if you don't need to know there is no way I'm telling*", "*as stealth as possible*", "*I just want to be a normal cis guy*" and so on. For people who were stealth and passed as male or had transitioned as male, they sometimes explained that they wanted to be received fully as a man: "*I don't want to be known as a trans, I want to be known as a man. Nothing else, just a man*". Several mentioned that coming out meant being analysed for signs of femininity, which made them uncomfortable: "I *don't want people picking the feminine features out and chucking them in my face*" said one, "*Some people start trying to find ways they might have been able to tell (e.g. small hands, no Adams apple)*" said another. Others worried they would not be treated "*as every man is treated*".

One participant who was stealth about their gender identity and still presented as female to some friends and family, explained on the discussion-board forum that being older and less distinct in identity meant it was particularly difficult to come out:

> I'm stealth because I'm having a hard time sticking a label on how I feel. I'm also probably older than some of the guys here, who are talking about how their parents reacted, so that means a lot of history with people. When I was in my 20s, even 30s, there was no information. I guess silence means I always am referred to as female and treated that way… it always feels wrong to me. Sometimes I find myself feeling angry with people for no good reason, or at least, no reason they know, because they have made a big deal of "girls together" or some such. A couple of close friends know, this is all. They have also come out as gender-fluid (labels again) so they are completely accepting. So no one has changed their treatment of me because they haven't had a chance to. My mother is in her 80s, very conventional and I know would not accept such a thing at all… even if she could understand it, which I doubt.

There was a sense for some genderqueer participants that coming out was optional, although others found their non-conforming differences were quite visible and explanations were sometimes demanded by rude strangers.

Some participants expressed guilt about going stealth. For example, one said he would like to come out as having a transgender history, but "*now that I am perceived as male I am never given a good opportunity to come out*". He wanted to be open so that he could raise awareness in his community. He explained, "*I feel that being stealth is an easy way out and it makes me feel guilty to fit in so easily when others can't.*" In the past he had experienced bullying, harassment, getting kicked out of male bathrooms and other incidents which had made stealth become his general mode of being. Stealth was a complex concept: it could be applied to different parts of one's identity (gender identity or lived experience, gender future, gender history, or general transgender status). It could be used to please one's self, or one's family, or amongst strangers. For example, one younger participant was currently going stealth about having a male gender identity (as they did not "pass" as male anyway), but intended to go stealth as a male after transition in the future. In some ways, being stealth in one area (about one's gender identity) might simply mean being honest in another (one's current embodiment), and vice versa. So the term probably sounds more "duplicitous" than it really is given the complexity of identity for FtM transgender people, and the different truths they experience about themselves. Being stealth was sometimes simply "the safest form of honest" available to someone in a particular time or place in their life.

Patterns in Social Life

As previously mentioned the respondents' satisfaction with their social life indicated that just over half were satisfied (55 %), approximately a third were dissatisfied (32 %) and some indicated that they felt neutral about their social life (14 %). Notably, family relationships were the most tense and difficult for the respondents to navigate with respect to their gender identity and the matter of acceptance. This was highlighted by awkward social interactions with family members, family members distancing themselves from their FtM relative, family members refusing to use new pronouns and names for their relative and/or efforts to try and keep trans-identity a secret. Some had experienced violence and broken contact altogether. Draconem (whose situation was discussed above) commented, "*Urgh. I've always had trouble with my family (except dad)*".

Harry (FtM transgender 24 years) described family relations as "distant", which was a term several people used about their families. He expanded: "*I don't speak to my father and his side of the family. My sibling and I are not close and they will not use my chosen name*". Zbdsm (male, 57 years) explained that his sister never accepted his decision and cut all contact. However, his niece recently connected with him and is very accepting. His daughter and grandchildren knew, but his youngest grandson had not been told because "*he is only 15* years *and can't keep a secret*". Other people discussed mothers who "*could lay a guilt trip on like the best of them*", fathers who walked out on them, siblings who limited contact to Facebook and so on. There were also passive-aggressive relatives who were known to "*remark on (male clothing) unfavourably*", or refuse to discuss issues.

Although many had tense relationships with family, there were a few whose families were very open and willing to learn about and accept trans-identity. Jay said his family relationships were great, although he added "*I live approx 1200 kms away from any of my family, haha, that might help! No but seriously we are all quite close and I know they would do anything for me at the drop of a hat*". Lance (male/transsexual male, 40 years) said "*I am close to my mother who is a sole parent, she is supportive of me. My brother and his wife are also supportive of me*". Some participants used words like "excellent", "loving" and "supportive" about their family relationships, which contrasted with the first group's experience.

As for friendships, most participants felt highly supported by a small community of close friends. This could be because friends are most often chosen, and therefore can be selected based on their ability to be accepting and understanding of trans-identity. A few participants described having created their "own family", "extended family" or "second family" out of their best friends who loved them unconditionally when they come out as either initially gay or transgender. This helped them weather periods of ostracism from biological family members. Conor (male, queer, trans*, person of colour, 24 years) had "*a handful of close, intimate and supportive relationships that are built around reciprocity and generosity*". He felt loved, valued and appreciated. Beyond these intimate relationships, he also had a large group of people with whom he could engage socially. Brett (male/transgender male, 27 years) said "*I'm so lucky I have an amazing relationship with everyone in my life... I'm making some great new trans friends too*".

Although some had a network of queer peers, they still felt segregated because they did not fit neatly into the 'gay' or 'straight' categories. For example, Harry explained:

> I don't make friends easily. The ones I have I feel segregated from, either because they are 'gay women' or 'straight men'. I use quotation marks because they have used these terms to make distinctions between them and me.

Ramir commented on a new set of connections he had sought out for extra support:

> I recently made some trans* friends and that really felt fulfilling and necessary. I found myself feeling quite isolated despite by wonderful cis friends. I felt I needed to talk about all the stuff that was on my mind with people that had been or were going through it. I also found the internet helped massively with this. Especially instagram and the large trans* community there. I have developed a lot as a person since connecting to people around the world who embrace everything trans*.

Al (masculine identified, 21 years) said that he copped "*snide remarks from lesbians*" and a lack of acceptance from other trans people because he was masculine identified.

Further, there were instances in which respondents lost friends or social support following disclosure of their identity. In addition, some respondents indicated that while they did have friends, the relationships were not satisfying or close. Having fewer friends may have been used as a defence against experiencing more discrimination and prejudice. Zbdsm spoke of spending many nights alone in his room, and Darkneko said "*I have a few friends but what we have is not a 'friendship', something like being in a relationship with a lover but without the love or sexual desire*". Other people responded with phrases like "*What social relationships???*", "*shallow*", "*superficial*" and "*standoffish*" to describe their difficult relationships with former or barely-there friends. Some had found they were not treated or accepted as male, genderqueer or in the way they identified.

With respect to intimate relationships, many respondents indicated that they were not seeing anyone. Some of those who were not in an intimate relationship indicated that they would like to be but were concerned about the completeness of their transition. Harry said he was pretty self-conscious about his body "*due to being pre op and I'm also still adjusting to the genital growth*". He was afraid that since most people had not been with a "trans dude" before, they would be "*judging my junk*". Jay similarly expressed that his intimate relationships were non-existent; "*People intrigue me and pique my interest but again I don't feel whole so I don't really engage in dating rituals*". Others seemed satisfied with not being in a relationship, saying they were not interested. Darkneko said "*I don't do romantic relationships. I don't make that connection with others*", whilst Eric (FtM transgender, 49 years) said "*I am basically not interested in sex, but spent quite a few unhappy years trying to date and be in relationships, with no success, due to my wish to fit in*". He had become aware of his own variations and discovered that friendship was more important for his personality.

Those who were in an intimate relationship indicated high levels of satisfaction, understanding, love and happiness. Conor was currently in a monogamous relationship that felt "*healthy, reciprocal and respectful*". He explained that both partners took on "*the work of the relationship*", and had articulated a level of commitment that made him feel secure and valued. Aid (socially male, 18 years) said his partner "*understands me and my struggles and always supports and loves me*". Ramir was in a romantic relationship that was very satisfying and full of love. He felt lucky that she understand him completely and accepted him. "*She is excited about my transition and is 100 % with calling me 'he' around other people... I am grateful that she hasn't been at all reluctant*". She was very patient and willing to explain things to people which made his transition process easier. Lance called his fiancé amazing: "*she is extremely supportive and embraces this journey with me*". However, a few people described partners who had stopped being supportive, or who had initially been supportive but then had withdrawn that support over time as the realities of changes to their relationship became challenging.

Positive Experiences

While most of the respondents experienced difficulties consolidating their gender-identity and their social lives many had received support. This support came mostly from friends but also family, health professionals and/or queer-safe spaces. Draconem recounted:

> My house-mate has been ever supportive and given me many tips for doing things as a man, without him I don't know how I would be. He has been my rock and guiding light, even when his own issues make him depressed, he has time for me. I am ever in his debt.

Jon Snow declared:

> My fiance still wants to marry me! When I came out to her at first she was angry. I think this was because it complicated her own sexual identity. She said 'Well now I'm not a lesbian, what does it make me?'... But she came around and is very supportive. She is my best friend and I trust her but it still scares me to think: what if she'd left me?

Maddox came out publicly through uploading a video onto his Facebook page to "*hit a few birds with one stone*". He had so much positive feedback "*from friends and family close and not close, all over the world*". He had continued to have people reach out to him online.

Other people described supportive doctors and helpful queer youth counsellors. Doc79, on the other hand, said that one of the best moments he had experienced (besides getting married and being there at the birth of his child) was when a gay man had asked him out. "*I felt like, well if he couldn't tell – I have nothing to worry about!*" He kindly turned down the offer, but said "*it was flattering (more than he will ever know)* ". He reflected:

> My partner has known from the start and she is wonderful. She has helped me so very much. All my family know and I've only had an amazing amount of support. Dad doesn't like to talk about it but has told me that he's proud. All my friends know and are the same as my family. I feel extremely lucky to have the people in my life that I have. They have only been supportive, interested and proud.

Future Supports

The previously outlined data indicate that education and advocacy about trans-identity is necessary in order for social networks to be more accepting, understanding and non-judgemental of difference (including queer organisations). The respondents also offered a few suggestions in their own words on how society could promote support and inclusion for FtM transgender people:

- I would like to see (and be a part of) talks in primary schools about transgender issues and acceptance, and talks in high schools about acceptance.
- Better legal rights recognition, and all government funded agencies/services have to do mandatory gender diversity awareness training.
- Other things I would like to see is better (and compulsory) inclusion of trans* and intersex people, our needs and specific health and cultural sensitivity issues in the medical school curriculum (rather than a one sentence brush-off under Psychiatry), and in allied health curriculum as well. At present there is limited coverage from biased people who aren't themselves part of the trans* and gender diverse community, and it's not compulsory to attend the lectures (and/or they are not assessed). We can't improve awareness and knowledge of health professionals without education from the earliest stages of training process! Specialists, GPs and allied health all need awareness.

- I did a talk at university once, to pre-med students. It was great… the questions were respectful, and it was positive to know I was helping inform people that we just have a medical condition and need some help like other people with medical conditions.
- Local queer youth workers are needed.
- I have loved going to a boys group and making some trans* friends, who are all very different to one another but great friends… I still felt quite isolated about my transness and have found a lot of solace in meeting other guys. It helped me to accept myself more- by celebrating them and their gender identity, and getting to know them as people. It has been a wonderful experience. It was also great for my partner to meet some trans* people and see that the path doesn't have to be as difficult and painful as we had possibly imagined.
- I would LOVE for there to be more of an equal representation of transgender people at the gay and lesbian Mardi Gras parade! Also I believe EDUCATION is the best form of activism! There should be more education on LGBTQI people in primary and high schools, to help stop bullying and to make those young rainbow people feel more comfortable in coming out!

Chapter 11
Sexuality, Romance and Relationships

Abstract Transgender people enliven sexualities research and can challenge traditional ideas about gender-based orientations or the mechanics of pleasure. This chapter examines data on sexuality, romance and relationships generated by the 273 FtM transgender Australians in the 2013 *E-Males* study. Over half of the participants were in a romantic/sexual relationship. Most had never married. Over one third of the *E-males* participants were attracted to both sexes and a quarter were attracted to people of the opposite sex. Many were attracted to all gender expressions, or challenged traditional "orientations". The commencement of medical transition sometimes enabled greater sexual engagement due to increased libido and bodily comfort. FtM transgender people engaged in unpredictable variations on a broad range of sexual behaviours with varying risk levels, from kissing and giving oral sex using latex protections, through to receiving various types of penetrative sex without protection; revealing a need for tailored sexual health information.

Keywords Transgender · FtM · Visibility · Media · Rights · Law · Research · Theory · Studies · Post-modern

> Defining my sexual orientation has always been somewhat confusing for me personally. As female born and as a teenager, realising I was attracted to girls and then to women, I was a lesbian (hate labels). Now as a mature aged transman who has had top surgery, but still has female sex organs in a way, I guess I see myself as a straight man with a twist. Currently there is no one in my life who rocks my world, so my current sex life is on hold. However when I was younger I had a few affairs of the heart, but nothing serious. During my transition and currently to this day my sex life is on hold, but I am willing if that special someone came along (Alex, male/transguy, straight with a twist, 22 years).

> I am attracted to men, women, intersex individuals, transsexuals and genderqueer or questioning. Gender is not important for me. I have had sex with men as a female presenting person, and women as both female and male presenting. Before transition I was unable to be touched by hands or mouths on my genitals and was unable to undress in front of others or a mirror. After t and chest surgery, I enjoy an active sex life that involves oral sex as well as penetrative sex. I am no longer uncomfortable being naked in front of others (Aid, Socially male, Pansexual, 18 years).

T. Jones et al., *Female-to-Male (FtM) Transgender People's Experiences in Australia*, SpringerBriefs in Sociology, DOI 10.1007/978-3-319-13829-9_11

Key Findings

- Almost half of the group were in monogamous relationships.
- The majority had never married.
- Over one third of the *E-males* participants were attracted to both sexes and a quarter were attracted to people of the opposite sex. There were also gay, pansexual, fluid and other sexual orientations.
- Some of those who were "lesbian" prior to transition, continued to be attracted to women but referred to themselves a "straight men" post-transition.
- Some transgender men were comfortable with a wide variety of sexual behaviours.
- For some, being transgender had created self-doubt about sexual relationships, but for others the commencement of medical transition prompted them to become more sexually active.

Relationship Status

Most of the participants were in a relationship: 43 % were in a monogamous relationship, 12 % were in an open relationship, and 5 % were in a polyandrous relationship. In addition, 8 % were single and dating, and a third (33 %) were single and not dating (Fig. 11.1).

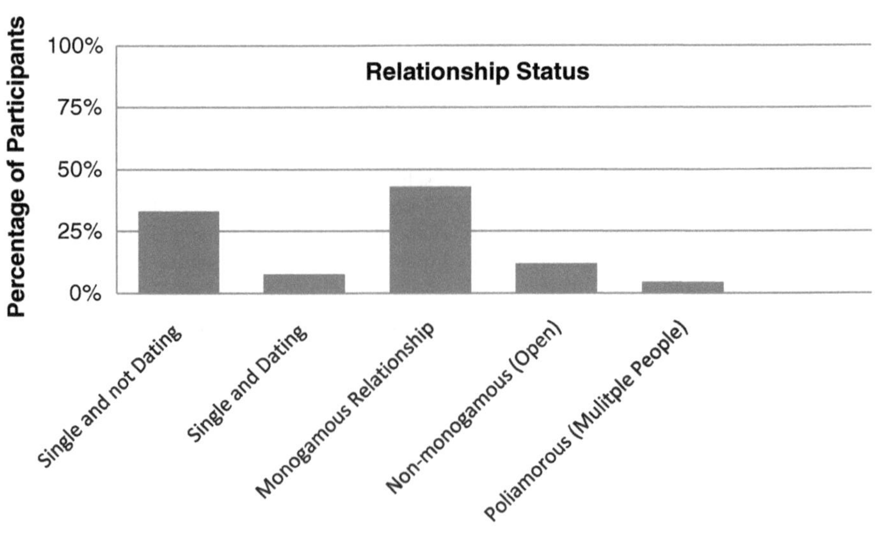

Fig. 11.1 Relationship status of *E-males* participants (n = 222)

Some participants had met their partner before they started transitioning. They transitioned during the course of the relationship and remained together, with the other partner being supportive throughout the process. For example, Maddox (male/ftm/transman, queer/heterosexual, 21 years) had found that this romantic and sexual dynamic with his girlfriend remained unchanged, despite the way the labels around it might have:

> I am in a long-term relationship with a woman. It is every bit as normal as any other heterosexual relationship; we have very heterosexual sex and always have. We have been together two and a half years, I have just moved interstate to be with her. We were together while I redefined my gender identity, so for the first two years we were titled "lesbians", but she has always felt I was her boyfriend and has always known this path would be the one I ended up on so she was ready for it. She has been one of my main supports. I prefer not to define my sexuality, but to myself or people close to me that were more understanding of sexual fluidity I would say just queer, but generally heterosexual is the best to describe it to others.

Nikozilar (male, bisexual/pansexual, 20 years) had felt particular support from his long-term boyfriend during the harder parts of transition:

> I had a few barely-anything relationships in my young teens with boys and girls. I tried to lose my virginity when I was 14 but it didn't go down too well – I was extremely upset about my body. Aged 17, I started dating my current partner (a male). We met at a LGBTI event and he saw me as male from the start. It's taken a while, but I feel very comfortable having sex with him. We've happily been together for years now and he helped me stay sane during the long wait to start testosterone.

Marital Status

When this study took place in 2013, Australia did not have equal marriage laws in place for GLBTIQ people broadly, although marriage activism across the community was strong. The then upcoming election had seen an assurance from Prime Minister Kevin Rudd and the Labor Party that he would support marriage equality within 100 days if re-elected, and from the Greens Party. There had been some inclusion of FtM transgender Australians, and some exclusion, in the Australian legal construction of "marriage". Criteria such as sex allocated at birth, life experiences, self-perception "as man or woman", sex reassignment procedures undertaken, and characteristics at the time of marriage were taken into consideration in regards to whether or not they could marry ("The Attorney-General for the Commonwealth v. "Kevin and Jennifer" and Human Rights and Equal Opportunity Commission" 2003). Essentially, FtM transgender people legally recognised as men could get married to a woman, but could not for example marry (or maintain a legal marriage) to a man. Intersex people did not have legal rights around marriage except in relation to achieving a heterosexual marriage as either a male or a female.

Therefore, it was not surprising that despite the "eligible" age of the group (the average age being 30) the majority had never married (two third or 66 %), and 18 %

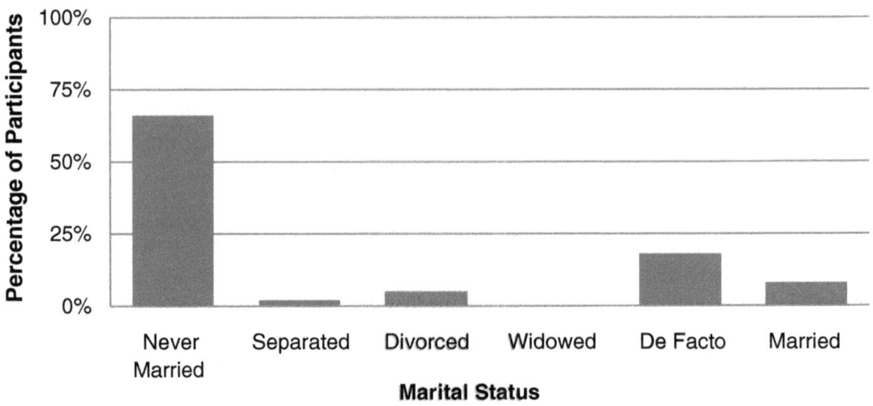

Fig. 11.2 The marital status of *E-males* participants (n = 222)

were in de facto relationships. Smaller groups had engaged in legal marriages either prior to or after transition—8 % were married, 5 % were divorced, and 2 % were separated (Fig. 11.2). There were also individuals within the de facto group who were engaged to be married in the future—either when they had transitioned (and thus could fit their relationships within the current laws), or when the law changed (to allow for their queer relationships). Lance (male/transsexual male, straight, 40 years) defined himself as heterosexual, and was attracted to femininity. He was in a relationship with a woman and they were engaged, and would be able to marry when he proceeded with his legal transition.

Sexual Orientation

In the survey, more than one third of the participants (36 %) reported being sexually attracted to people of both sexes; one quarter (25 %) was attracted to the opposite sex, 15 % reported they were same sex attracted, 14 % expressed that their sexual attraction changed and 10 % were not certain (Fig. 11.3). On the discussion-board forum blog, the participants delivered a variety of responses to the topic of sexual identity which clearly revealed intricate aspects of transgender sexuality which defy the boundaries of rigid orientation alignments. The answers in regards to sexual attraction could be grouped under categories of attraction towards: "male-born men and transmen"; "female-born and transwomen"; "only women"; "only men"; "both sexes"; "all gender expressions" and "specific persons regardless of their anatomy or gender identity". One person expressed being "undefined" in regards to his sexual orientation. Others expressed a sexual orientation for which single labels were not available. For example, Both/Other (male, 51 years) said:

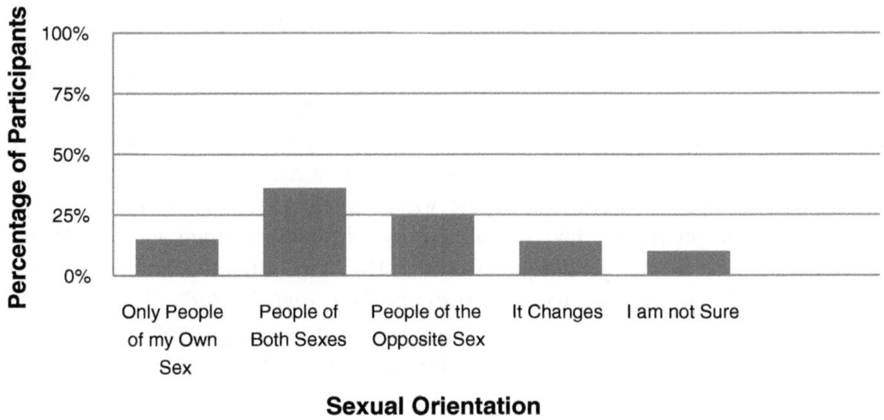

Fig. 11.3 Sexual orientation of the *E-males* participants (n = 212)

> I am attracted to both sexes, but mostly only gay people in those categories, and only the more "masculine" in demeanor of those categories. Some gay males, some "butch" lesbians. Also some androgynous-type of people – again, those who are more "masculine" in demeanor. I am never attracted to "femme" (i.e. distinctly feminine in demeanor), regardless of how they themselves identify in terms of both gender and sexuality. I am not attracted to the majority of lesbian women, nor straight women. Some straight men attract me, but not often. Seems that a "queer" energy twist is key, along with masculine-type energy.

Many participants referred to fluctuations throughout their lives in the choice of sexual partners. Some expressed that despite always having been in relationships with women (pre- and post-transition), they would always identify as "queer" because they were attracted to all expressions of gender despite their current or past circumstances in relationships. For example, Ramir (transgender, homo/queer, 25 years) was open to falling for anyone, but thus far had only been with cis-women. He was now in a long-term relationship, and hoped to be with her "*for the long run*". However, he identified as "Homo/queer"; "*I feel strongly that I am not straight even if I am in a guy-girl relationship. My lesbian community is a big part of my life*". He said he considered himself "*queer 100 %*", and his current girlfriend "*accepts me for the person that I am, and that includes treating me accordingly in the bedroom according to what I am comfortable/uncomfortable with*".

Sexual Identity

Those attracted to "all expressions of gender" on the discussion boards described themselves as gay, queer, pansexual or bisexual. This was the largest group. Sometimes the terminology used by this group depended on context; it was sometimes felt necessary to erase more complicated elements of sexual identity and history in particular environments where people had restricted understanding of the potential complexity of identity. For example, Garfield (male, 31 years) was in a permanent monogamous relationship with a man, so he tended to describe himself as "gay" to the broader community, as it was easier for them to understand given their acceptance of him as male and his current relationship as therefore gay in mainstream thinking. But if he was describing his attractions to others within the queer community, he tended to use the word "*queer (usually PDQ, pretty darn queer)*". He had previously had sexual activity with men, women and people who defined themselves as genderqueer/trans*. He was attracted to "*all gender expressions, the whole spectrum of presentations and bodies*". The disruptive elements to his gender identity and history, sexual past and present were all more readily understood in queer contexts, so he was more comfortable activating those elements to his identity therein.

Both/Other also came under this group, and classed his homosexually-focused bi-sexuality as "pansexual" (with some uncertainty). JW (Male/ftm/slightly Genderqueer, pansexual 19 years) said he was attracted to femininity through to masculinity, and that "*I fall in love with the person rather than their parts or identity*". In general he was more likely to be attracted to female-identified people's personalities. He had had monogamous relationships with males "*when seen as a straight woman*", and monogamous and polyamorous relationships with women "*when seen as a lesbian*". Darkneko (FtM transgender, bisexual, 21 years) was bisexual and attracted to all expressions of gender, with a preference towards females. "*I could date anyone that caught my eye,*" he noted, "*regardless of gender or how they expressed it or dressed it*".

Those attracted to "only women" generally described themselves as straight. Within this group some had defined themselves as lesbians before transition. For example, Jay (male, 30 years) said:

> I am a straight man. I have only ever been involved with women. Prior to transition I lived as a 'lesbian' and I dated mostly straight women. They all said that I was the exception.

Brett (male/transgender male, 27 years) said was a 'lesbian' before he started his transition and "*very much loved the ladies*". He maintained no attraction to males what so ever, and was attracted to femininity. He had been sexually active since 17, and had only been with women. He had found his current partner three and a half years ago.

Those attracted to "only males" and "males and transmen" described themselves as gay. For example Draconem (FtM transgender, gay, 24 years) said he was "*attracted to men, this seems to include transmen - make of that what you will*". He saw his identity as "gay" and had been with two guys prior to coming out as male. He explained that "*one knows, the other doesn't. Neither were gay*". He said that his revelation made his most recent ex "*freak out a bit; he's very much not gay*". Draconem hadn't tried to get a partner since coming out as male, mostly because he felt he'd have "*no idea how to go about it*". Looking into his sexual history further, he reflected that his gay identity felt like a "fit" with who he partnered with and the way he partnered with them online:

> I've had multiple online sexual encounters, starting at around the age of 13 and continuing until the age of 17. During this time I never 'performed' on webcam or showed photos of myself to my partners.

Conor (male, queer, trans*, person of colour, gay/queer, 24 years) was attracted to men, predominantly, clarifying that he did not make a distinction between men and trans men. He was attracted to masculine, feminine, and all variables of men, and said "*I like when men own their gender*". He called himself "gay/queer", and was currently in a relationship with a cis man, but they wanted to have a threesome. In the past, he had mainly had sexual relations with cis men, but had experienced a short sexual relationship with a woman.

Impact on Sexual Life

Brett felt that his transsexuality had not affected his sexual relationship at all. He engaged in the same sexual acts—kissing, performing oral sex, receiving oral sex, performing penetrative sex through the front hole (vaginal) on his partner, and wearing a strap on—and was with the same partner in roughly the same dynamic. Similarly, in considering if being FtM transgender had impacted his sex life, Conor said, "*I don't think it has impacted it*". Albeit, he acknowledged that he had historically had "*a lot of anxiety about new partners interacting with my junk*", but that in his current relationship he did not. Overall, he felt that, "*if anything, it has helped because we don't have to worry about preparing for penetrative sex beforehand*" (he meant this in regards to protection, which he was no longer using, believing he could not get pregnant on testosterone). Similarly, *Maddox* said his relationship with his girlfriend had been still very heterosexual when he was considered a "lesbian", and the sex had a similar aesthetic after transition:

> It hasn't changed my sex life all that much, me and my partner always had very heterosexual sex. When I started T my sex drive went up extremely and that has so far been very positive. It has also helped to understand why certain things make me uncomfortable during sex. Knowing that dysphoria is normal for transgender people helps my partner and I.

He engaged in kissing, performing oral sex, receiving oral sex both with or without his prosthetic penis, performing vaginal and anal sex, and wearing a strap-on (although he preferred his own prosthetic penis). They used condoms, "*for prevention of anything; the idea of prevention of pregnancy is nice for us*".

For some their sexuality had been affected since they became aware of their trans* identity, as had their ability to have relationships. JW said "*Null and void: I have had no relationships since being out as trans*". Thewaywesee (trans* male or queer male, pansexual, 22 years) said "*What sexual life? It was hard enough finding* *someone when seen as female. Now being a trans* male I don't even know where to begin*". Thewaywesee was attracted to all gender expressions, including masculinity in female identified people and the femininity in male identified people in particular. In the past, when he was seen as female he was in one long term relationship with a man, and also had a few sexual relationships with women. "*Since coming out as trans* I haven't been with anyone,*" he declared. Jay found that his previous ease with relationships had been damaged since he had realised he did not feel complete:

> Being a transsexual man had impacted greatly – I don't feel like I can be with someone when I myself don't feel whole. I don't feel like I can just pick someone up like a normal guy and take them home. I would (ideally) engage in kissing, giving and receiving oral, performing penetrative sex through the front hole, wearing a strap-on. Honestly to date – nothing:/.

However, he remained hopeful and prepared: "*I now have condoms on standby*".

Junk000 (male, undefined, 22 years) was originally attracted to feminine males. However, now he could not give a label to his sexual orientation. He had found that recognising his gender identity impacted his sexual life (and subsequently, his identity) in two ways:

> The first, it has obliterated it – as while my gender identity didn't exist, I also wasn't afraid of people's reactions once they found out I wasn't, how would you say, conventionally bodied – that is, either reacting hostilely or with disgust, or otherwise exposing me, or seeking me only for novelty. The second, I suddenly became attracted to women? I can't work it out beyond sexual fluidity, but I think it has something to do with reading sexual come-ons from women as directed at me instead of at other people, and that made a massive difference.

Alex800 (transman, straight, 48 years) was attracted to femininity, particularly "*a woman who looks sexy in a pair of jeans and super sexy in a dress*". Defining his sexual orientation was always somewhat confusing for him, and his transition had impacted how he labelled and acted on his sexual life:

> As female born and as a teenager, realising I was attracted to girls then later to women I was a lesbian (hate labels). Now as a mature aged transman who has had top surgery, but still has female sex organs, in a way I guess I see myself as a straight man with a twist.

Others found that realising their FtM identity more fully had marked an improvement in their sexual life. Doc79 (male, straight, 33 years) was attracted to femininity in female born and transwomen, and understood himself as a straight man. He said that prior to his transition sex was almost non-existent. "*I didn't want to be touched really… didn't want to be naked, looked at or even look at myself*", he detailed. He had one male sexual partner prior to transition which he described as "*boring as watching paint dry*". He had one female partner prior to transition which he considered awkward, as he had urges to perform as a male. He clarified this; "*not sure how to put this… umm… I wanted to pretend I had a real penis and not want to act as though it was a lesbian relationship*". After starting T hormones, his sex life increased a little. After undergoing surgeries he really began to be more comfortable about walking around his house naked, and he started feeling better about his body. "*Sex became easier because I was more confident*", he explained.

Now he had a wife of 10 years and said, "*we do what we do, without a lot of variation*". He explained that he still needed a strap-on as his phalloplasty is without an erectile device and is "*not able to be bound or anything to be used for sex, just there for show*". However, for Doc79 realizing that he was trans* helped him to better understand what he previously considered sexual problems or blockages, and realize that his discomfort was with his body rather than with sex. For example, he disliked attention to his breasts, felt uncomfortable with vaginal penetration, and felt like sex in a certain manner was inherently wrong for him. Yet he had also felt that other sexual behaviors which "*wouldn't usually feel right for a biological female*" were inherently right for him.

Gavin (male/FtM transgender, straight, 23 years) was attracted to feminine women and defined as heterosexual. He had a few sexual relationships and some non-sexual relationships with men when he was in high school, just before coming out, but they were all short-lived. Once he came out he had sexual relationships with women. He felt transitioning had changed his sexual life:

> With women that do know about me (gender) I would say yes (my sex life has changed) because I have a tendency to perform like a guy, but with girls that don't know about me I will try to hold back in that sense.

Aid (socially male, pansexual, 18 years) said that he was attracted to "*men, women, intersex individuals, transsexuals and genderqueer or questioning*" as gender was not important for him. Describing himself as pansexual, he reported that he had had sex "*with men as a female-presenting person and women as both female- and male-presenting*". Before transition he was "*unable to be touched by hands or mouths on my genitals, and was unable to undress in front of others or a mirror*". After testosterone treatments and chest surgery, he said "*I enjoy an active sex life that involves oral sex as well as penetrative sex*". He said he is no longer uncomfortable being naked in front of others, but now "*comfortable with all*".

Hansel (genderqueer, queer, age 22 years) reflected that his main attraction was personalities, be it masculine girls, feminine boys, and those inside or none of that. "*I like someone who is fabulous and beautiful inside and out, it all gets down to how we connect*" he explained. His current relationship had just been renegotiated. He had a flexible partner who understood his need to explore his own identity and boundaries throughout his transition, and was willing to adapt:

> I've been with my current (first proper relationship) partner for over a year now. We have a great relationship and have just discussed being in an open relationship after discussing polyamory etc. Meaning we are open to dating others, which I think is good for her with my physical changes happening, as long as we are open about it and communicate well. When we first met, she could tell I was struggling with gender identity etc. and said it wouldn't matter to her if I was a girl a boy or anything else, and she is very thoughtful about the anxieties I may have personally and sexually etc. So there is no "self-consciousness". She does identify as "queer" because she has been attracted to people who do not identify as "female" (myself being one), but she is generally attracted to female identified people, and she herself is also very attracted to personalities. I do not know what's ahead of me in this relationship, but I know it is right for us, and we will take the hurdles as they come. Before starting T I had no libido whatsoever. Now after starting I actually know what it means to

> have a sex drive ☺. Oh and the only other thing I can think of, I'm always scared when someone asks for my number at a bar because I don't know if they think I'm a boy or a girl (that never used to phase me).

Sexual Expressions

We asked the participants about the sexual acts they felt comfortable engaging in, given the right circumstances or partner. For some participants it was difficult to discuss sexual acts using cis-gendered frames of their bodies. Mr Dude (transsexual male, 22 years) helpfully explained that in discussing sexual expression it was important to use particular terminology for his body parts. "*I don't have a vagina,*" he explained, "*I have a bonus hole. Other names that don't make me cringe are boy hole and front hole*". Other participants discussed conceptualising their body parts with similar agency, but in different ways—using front holes as back holes, using body parts or strap-ons as a phallus for example. There were participants interested in bringing bodies together in all sorts of creative ways, alongside participants who didn't particular enjoy sex or being touched.

We listed some possible sexual acts to stimulate the discussions:

- none,
- kissing,
- performing oral sex,
- receiving oral sex,
- performing penetrative sex through the front hole (vaginal)
- receiving penetrative sex through the front hole (vaginal)
- performing penetrative sex anal,
- receiving penetrative sex anal,
- wearing a strap on,
- anything,
- other.

Several participants responded quite positively to the list on the whole. Draconem said, "*I'll go with 'anything' including 'other'. Haha.*" Garfield joked that he'd happily engage in "*all of the ones you listed except for 'none'*". Both/Other said, "*Anything*". Conor said he'd done all of the above except performing penetrative anal sex and wearing a strap on. He would probably feel comfortable doing other things—e.g. engaging in kink—if his boyfriend wanted to try something. JW would do everything on the list except anal, because those things "*feel good*". Several participants expressed an openness to practice all kinds of sexual behaviours, making statements like "*I'll try anything once*". *Photoman* (male, 41 years) was attracted to both femininity and masculinity, and defined his sexual orientation as bisexual. He had been married for 14 years, and had a boring sex life where "*doggy style was the most adventurous position*". Then he had another long term relationship with a MTF transgender woman, a "*very adventurous sexual relationship*", and the most recent was with a female who preferred the missionary position. He was open to many sexual possibilities in the future.

Nikozilar said that being attracted to both/all sexes, he was attracted to "*all combos of gender + gender expression*". He identified as bisexual/pansexual and yet sometimes felt more gay or more straight. He said he had taken a long time to be able to do much with another person due to his body discomfort, but that since he'd been transitioning and taking testosterone he had been feeling a lot better and had developed a "*massive libido... which helps things along*". He had done everything on the list of sexual acts mentioned quite comfortably, and had found that receiving (anal) sex from his boyfriend was "*the most normal-feeling sexual act for me apart from normal foreplay stuff*".

There were others—particularly those who identified as straight males—who were less interested in experimentation or in receiving penetrative sex. However there were also straight males interested in receiving penetration. Darkneko was one of the individuals less interested in sex even more broadly, saying he would consider kissing and giving oral to a woman only, and was not particularly keen to. As the discussion board group on this question was a small sample (21 answered this particular question), what can be learned from this is only that some FtMs are willing to try anything once, others are less so. No general rules of preference for the group should be declared. It is noteworthy however that FtM Australians may engage in a broader range of behaviours than sexual health providers and sex educators might assume, and with a variety of partners.

Sexual Protection

International research has suggested that STD and HIV infection can be high for some FtM communities (Kenagy and Hsieh 2005; Rowniak et al. 2011; Stephens et al. 2011). The literature mentioned contributing factors such as high risk sexual behaviours, hyper sexuality and genital dryness/bleeding during hormone therapy, the unfamiliar nature of the gay community for men who had sex with men, and incorrect assumptions concerning risk. We explored how the *E-males* participants protected themselves during sexual engagements on our discussion board forums.

In the international literature, it was argued that sometimes FtM transgender people were under-prepared for their new level of sexual risk, particularly within gay male communities (who generally had more established knowledge about sexual practices and protection options). This appeared to be the case for most of the participants on the discussion board. Of the 21 who responded to this question, the majority were not using any form of protection. One showed typical thinking of the group when he reasoned that with his boyfriend he would no longer need protection against pregnancy "*as that cycle isn't happening any more*". He also expressed a very common belief (particularly amongst gay and pansexual participants) when he assumed that he didn't need to use protection against STIs because he was in a long term relationship with a cis-man "*and we've both been tested multiple times such that we're confident that isn't an issue for us. Bonus!*". Similarly, another said that he and his partner used to use condoms before they both had sexual health tests, but now that they were both in the clear they did not use anything.

Several others (who had most recently been in relationships with women before becoming trans) used no protection at all—a practice quite common amongst lesbian communities, and which seemed to be "exported" from lesbian experiences into FtM sexual lives post-transition. However, this exportation of a low-risk assumption was not just carried over by the FtM transgender men themselves. One said that when he had gone to a doctor for an STD test (as an FtM transgender person who had only slept with women), the doctor had laughed and tried not to give him one—suggesting as with lesbians that he was at no risk at all. This simply is not true—oral and vaginal sex can on their own transmit chlamydia and herpes for example, amongst other STDs. The data showed further that there is a potential for sexual exploration and different sexual behaviours amongst different FtM transgender populations who do not all identify as "heterosexual men" and "ex-lesbians", but sometimes—as with some of our participants—engaged in an unpredictable range of high risk activities such as receiving anal without protection as a main sexual activity.

Whilst some of the participants felt they were making safe choices given the tests they were taking in their monogamous relationships or their lack of sex, many had said they were open to new practices (such as threesomes, kink and so on), new sexual opportunities and experimenting. They, like several others whose sexual practices were varying as they embraced their gender identity, could use more information about protection compared to the types of information they had (or perhaps had not) been exposed to in the past (as presumed lesbian or heterosexual women). Precise information about pregnancy risk—and at which point this was lowered by gender treatments—would also be useful given some of the FtM men slept with cis-men, trans-women and others without any protection at various stages of their transitions.

Some of the other participants said they would and had protected themselves actively during sexual engagements, and described using condoms, gloves and latex barriers. Others were looking into their options for protection. Some were also considering engaging in play with new toys, bdsm, kink and other areas but did not feel they knew much about how to proceed. Given that these men had been seeing doctors and other health practitioners (in most cases) fairly often for their gender affirmations and transitions, these engagements seemed good opportunities for them to be provided with sexual health materials that could cover their broad range of potential needs and activities. However, the lack of FtM-focussed information on sexuality was clearly a barrier to such knowledge transmission, alongside doctors' lack of awareness of the varied sexual behaviours and risks of FtM transgender people.

Chapter 12
Parenting

Abstract This chapter explores the data on parenting from the 2013 *E-Males* study of 273 FtM transgender Australians. Some participants were parents or knew of other FtM transgender people who were. They expressed frustration that their ability to parent was widely overlooked, as it was an important element in their identity. FtM transgender people had become parents through having had their own biological children, through fostering and adoption, through their partners or other pathways. Some respondents who were not intending to have children had given serious consideration to egg donation, and others enjoyed having children in their lives through other means, such as being uncles to nephews and nieces. The question of disclosure (or not) of one's trans* status to one's children was considered challenging to navigate by some participants, with significant positives and negatives to either path of action. There was a growing need for more resources in this area.

Keywords Transgender · FtM · Parent · Father · Children · Baby · Family · Egg donation · Adoption · Fostering

> I have a three year old son. I want more but I am never falling pregnant again. It was the most excruciatingly painful (not just physical) nine months of my life. So I will leave the future kids to my fiancé! My son has no concept of gender anything at all. He thinks everyone has every private part. He says he is a girl and that myself and my fiancé are boys. I think he may have the words mixed up. He calls my facial hair "whiskers" just like granddad. As he grows I will explain everything to him (Jon Snow, male/trans guy, 23 years).

> I would love to be a Father- it's one of my biggest dreams. I cannot imagine how I would deal with, for one reason or another, not being able to become a Father. I'm not sure how I would explain (my gender identity) to my children when the time comes, it's something I haven't given much thought to as it's not an immediate issue. I guess I would just take it into consideration with my partner (Maddox, male/ftm/transman, 21 years).

T. Jones et al., *Female-to-Male (FtM) Transgender People's Experiences in Australia*, SpringerBriefs in Sociology, DOI 10.1007/978-3-319-13829-9_12

Key Findings

- Many FtM transgender people were parents, and expressed frustration that FtM transgender people are rarely constructed in that light.
- The *E-males* participants had become parents in a variety of different ways: through having had their own biological children, through fostering and adoption, through their partners and so on.
- Some respondents who were not intending to have children had given serious consideration to egg donation.
- The question of disclosure (or not) of one's trans* status to one's children was considered a challenging one to navigate by some participants, with significant pros and cons on both sides.
- There was a growing need for more resources in this area.

Parenting and Identity

There was a group of participants who were parents. For those participants, being a parent was a key part of (or even, in their minds, the most important part of) their identity, and a key role they experienced in their day-to-day life. It was also an identity aspect which they were keen for the study to explore. Early on in the life of the study, at least one of these participants had expressed frustration on our interactive discussion board forum blogs, and pointed out that we had not included any questions on issues of parenthood:

> The one thing I didn't see in the questionnaire was "do you have any children/want children in the future" and "how does this affect your relationships and social status"? I have a child and I was disappointed that this wasn't included. I think it is an important issue because it's always a question I get asked, especially from people who don't know about my past. It's like some people think trans*people don't have or want children. I also know a lot of FTM people with children, either biological or with their partners (Tom Goldon, male, 35 years).

Although we had not originally inquired into these issues, Tom's comment prompted us to add these types of questions to our online discussion board forum early on during the data collection phase of the project. Our hope was that he and our other participants could feel supported to discuss parenting; and identify themselves in this research as parents, fathers, uncles, foster parents or otherwise.

Becoming a Parent

When American man Thomas Beatie became pregnant in 2008 because his wife was unable to, the topic of FtM parenting was brought into the mainstream global limelight for the first time, with coverage in multiple newspapers, television news shows and even an Oprah special (Turner 2008). Whilst the urge for some transgender people to conform to normative masculine roles such as "husband and father" have been used by some theorists as signs of the conservative nature of transgender identity, the image of a pregnant man splashed over papers and television screens presented a significant, undeniably subversive visual disruption to the very core of gender as a binary construct. It showed that transgender identity was neither inherently normative nor inherently dissident. Beatie had not particularly sought to spark controversy in becoming pregnant, but neither was he afraid of it in fulfilling his family goals with his wife. He said that in his personal experience, becoming a parent was neither a male or female desire, but a "human" one. The sensationalised coverage of Beatie's story revealed what had been a more commonly known fact in transgender circles for some time; that FtM transgender people can be, and have been for many years, parents. Issues of family and parenting for FtM transgender people can present quite a challenge. The challenge is both for the men transitioning into the role of "parent/father" (which is for anyone its own learning experience), and for society in general (with its hierarchies of norms). FTM Australia's website had a page of resources on becoming a parent,[1] and some new books and journals had also emerged on the topic (such as the *Transgendered Parents and Parents-to-be's Journal*[2]).

E-males participants had become parents in a variety of different ways: through having had their own biological children prior to transition, through fostering and adoption, or through their partners for example. In addition, some respondents did not undergo a hysterectomy during transitioning or their own path to gender affirmation. They thus were potentially able to maintain the physical capability of bearing children themselves if they chose to have a child or if for example a future female partner was unable to conceive, or a future male partner conceived with them, or other possibilities arose. Some respondents had also opted to freeze their eggs prior to having a hysterectomy. In some Australian states (such as Victoria) having a hysterectomy had been required in order to have documentation amended for legal transitions, so for many participants having a hysterectomy or some form of sterilisation had not been a choice. Hysterectomies had also been broadly recommended for FtM people undergoing hormonal treatment, due to the increased risk of cervical cancer (Futterweit and Deligdisch 1986; Michel et al. 2001). Therefore, there were restrictions to the means by which some individual respondents could become parents, and in our limited data on this topic (21 posts on the discussion boards and some additional information given in the survey's qualitative data), the parents had most commonly either had their children prior to transition, or with a subsequent partner.

Jon Snow (male/trans guy, 23 years) had a 3 year old son prior to beginning his transition. He planned to have more children, but in the future it would be his new fiancé who would conceive and carry them. Doc79 (male, 33 years) had had one

[1] http://www.ftmaustralia.org/publications/parenting-and-family-resources.

[2] http://transparents.livejournal.com/.

child, pursuing IVF with his wife through donated sperm and his wife's eggs. He would like to have more, but his wife had fertility problems and could not conceive any more. He commented that IVF had become way too expensive over time. He felt that his gender history had impacted his approach to child-rearing, in that it allowed their family to be "a little more open to toys played with (girls and boys toys)". Zbdsm (male, 57 years) had a daughter prior to transition and now had grandchildren. Jbt2010 (male, 52 years) was an example of one of the participants who provided foster care for children, and was currently looking after one foster child during the period of the study.

Childless, Not Child-Free

Some of our participants described having no desire or intention to have children. A few negated the concept quite strongly on the discussion board forum, arguing that it would be socially irresponsible to have kids—although whether they meant this widely in regards to their transgender status, or were referring to their individual circumstances and lack of parenting skills or inclination, was sometimes unclear. What *was* clear in reviewing the respondents' comments on this topic was that the decision to have or not to have children was a thoughtfully considered one, with respondents on both sides of the debate taking into account the feelings and potential experiences of both the children and of the participants themselves. However, a number of the respondents falling into the category of "intentionally childless" reported that their lives were not completely child-free. Indeed, several enjoyed engaging in the role of "uncle" to their siblings' and partners' siblings' children.

These included junk000 (male, 22 years) who did not want children because it would be "*socially irresponsible and physically horrifying, coupled with the fact I just inherently do not get along with young children*". However, for Junk000 the sense that having children was socially irresponsible was not related to his transgender status, but to the sense that there were many kids without parents who needed homes, and he said he "*might consider adopting an older child in the distant future*". Brett (male/transgender male, 27 years) commented "*I don't have children and don't want children. But I'm going to be an uncle one day, and knowing that fills me with joy *smiley face**". Alex (19, male) had no children but said "*I do enjoy been the uncle to my sister's children*". Several other respondents discussed their enjoyment of playing with their nephews and nieces, younger cousins and friends children, and the way these children stopped their lives from being "child-free".

One of our participants also expressed no desire to have children of his own, but had considered egg donation to couples who are unable to have children. The general altruistic sentiment was, "I'm not going to use them, but maybe someone can":

> I don't have children, and I don't want to have or raise children. But I've thought about offering my oocytes (eggs) for donation, since I'm not planning to use them and I'm sure there are people out there who really want children and need them (preferably a queer couple). I understand that this would require for me to cease testosterone for up to a year to see if things start working again in that department, before I can donate them. This doesn't really bother me as it would be temporary and for a purpose. However, I'm not sure any IVF clinic would be prepared to take them… or even how to bring up the topic. I suppose I like the idea that a part of me would 'go on', in some way. Some gay men (born with testes) I have spoken with who feel this way have acted as sperm donors for lesbian couples, or donated to sperm banks. There are people out there who want children badly, but don't themselves have functional gametes. I have gametes that I'm not going to use. Seems like a no-brainer (garfield, male, 31 years).

Disclosure to Children

The topic of disclosure to children came up on the discussion board through the conversations of the participants. It was then added as a separate question by the researchers. We asked participants how they explained their gender identity and process of transformation to their own children, or to those of other members of their family. Some of the respondents either had already told the story of their gender to children, or planned to in the future. There was an emphasis on age appropriate information in their responses. For example, Garfield responded that in relation to his nephews and nieces, "*I was transitioned several years before they were born, and the issue hasn't arisen. I suspect if it did, we would probably just explain it in an age appropriate way*". Jon Snow's child was still a toddler and had not yet developed concrete concepts of gender, genitals or sex markers for different groups of people. Jon planned to "*explain everything to him*" as he grew older. He had the support of most of his wider family in the meantime.

However, some participants did not particularly want to discuss their gender identity or history with their children, and they tended to have several reasons informing that decision. For example, Doc79 said his child was going through assessments "*for autism, or maybe OCD*" and he and his wife were therefore having "*enough troubles with unusual behaviors without adding some more uncertainty to it*". He reflected that there was "*also another part of me that says if I tell someone else, it makes it real… and I try to hide my past as much as I can*". Coming out, even to one's child, could thus be seen as a dysphoric or painful experience for the parent themselves. There were cases where disclosure had not occurred directly, but was implied through acts of transition. For example Alex (male, 48 years) said, "*strange as it seems, I never did (disclose my transgender status)*". He explained that disclosing the process of his transition was not necessary as his gender identity was something everyone probably always knew about, from his tomboyish ways. No one in our sample stated categorically that they would *never* tell their own or other kids about their trans* status, and in some cases it had simply not yet become a pressing issue.

Disclosure to children sparked a spirited debate amongst participants, with strong feelings and opinions on both sides. Proponents for disclosure cited goals such as fighting prejudice and reducing stigma in their support of disclosure. It was notable that this comment came from a participant in his 20s who had no children, and who readily identified as transgender (rather than male as such):

> I find it really interesting that you wouldn't tell your child about your identity! I personally would want my kids to know, because I feel strongly about fighting prejudice and being visible as a good role model. I grew up somewhere where no one was even out as gay or lesbian, let alone trans*. So I grew up feeling extremely different, isolated, ashamed and unhappy. I know it's a personal choice of course...

Such comments showed that there were FtM transgender people who felt a responsibility to enhance visibility of transgender issues to children.

In defence of not disclosing, people generally argued that they were protecting their children and families from potential discrimination. It was poignant that the following comment came from a participant in his 30s who had a child, and who identified as male, but understood being transgender as a mental illness which he preferred not to discuss:

> How much stigma, and isolation and rejection have you faced as a trans person? I have faced it, lost friends, and am still losing family after 10 years. I don't need to make my child aware of my disease to teach my child to be accepting, tolerant and to not judge people. It is an attitude that is learnt from social settings (including family). I can teach my kid, 'Hey, they're gay, they're straight, they're trans'. But you know what? Who cares, we are all people. I do not want to be defined as just a trans person. I do not want my child to face ANYTHING I have faced. Same as people with all other mental illness, they don't go telling everyone they have it. They take their medication and get on with life. I can't change the opinions of every child at school who may or may not tease my child for having a parent that is different. But I can make the decision not to tell my child. 1: one less thing my child will have to deal with at school if the wrong child is told, and 2: I won't have to deal with 'you're not my dad' or being called a girl when my child gets angry... all kids get angry and sometimes say things they don't mean, I know that. All I can do is be the best parent I can, and right now I am CHOOSING not to tell my child, to protect my child from facing any of the crap I have had to face (Doc79, male, 33 years).

It appeared that in thinking about disclosure to children, people were informed by their own identity (as male or transgender), their own needs as a child (whether for more role models or for greater safety), social context, their child's age and abilities, and their ideals for family dynamics. There was no set rules, or established or agreed community perspective on the best path. Like many aspects of parenting, there were different theories on what was "best", and sensitivities around personal choices that had been made. More resources around FtM parenting could assist people in making the right decision for their particular situation. It would be useful for the resources to be pluralistic and affirming, in providing an understanding that there are many truths to the identities that FtM Transgender parents share with their children—whether they disclose to them their gender identity, gender history, or allocated birth sex or not.

Chapter 13
Conclusion and Recommendations

Abstract In concluding our discussion of the 2013 *E-Males* study of 273 FtM transgender Australians, this chapter outlines the key findings of the data. We urge all Australian government offices and other places where documentation (featuring name and sex) is required to familiarise staff with new national guidelines on the recognition of gender. We call for national education policy that includes guidelines around combatting transphobia and specific guidelines around issues like information provision, uniforms and bathrooms, and management plans. We recommend workplace equity training measures broadly, and training in gender identity issues for a range of other medical and health practitioners who may engage with FtM transgender Australians on various gender affirmation journeys. We highlight the need for consistency in provisions regardless of state, and the need for clearer standards based on research. Particular provisions for youth, genderqueer people and rural people are called for. Areas for further research are detailed.

Keywords Transgender · FtM · Recommendations · Policy · Guidelines · Training · Standards · Action · Research · Gap

> I haven't been able to find any gender identity clinics in this state and not even a counsellor, so far, so I can't give any information. I was hoping to get some through this study! (Eric, FtM transgender, age 49 years).

Trends and Individuals

There was no single "truth" to what it meant to be an FtM transgender Australian. There were certainly trends in identification and experiences. Many people saw themselves as male. Many people engaged in a transition of some kind and found it beneficial to their wellbeing. Many people were highly educated but had low incomes. Many people were satisfied with life in general but had experienced depression and anxiety. However, there were also subgroups and individuals with conflicting identification and experiences—people who primarily identified as

T. Jones et al., *Female-to-Male (FtM) Transgender People's Experiences in Australia*, SpringerBriefs in Sociology, DOI 10.1007/978-3-319-13829-9_13

transgender or were genderqueer, people who had not or did not wish to transition formally, people who left school early, had very high incomes, and so on. There were many people who had been exposed to quite affirming discourses on FtM transgender identity, and who expected that it was the role of society and its structures (schools, the workforce, services) to adapt, not themselves. But there were also people influenced by psycho-analytic and traditional frames of thinking who saw their FtM transgender status as a mental illness that should be kept hidden, and who wished that they could change that aspect of themselves.

There were people who lived their lives as "out and proud" advocates for the FtM transgender community, and people who "went stealth" (or did not out themselves as transgender) for periods of time or in particular contexts. There were fathers and foster parents, active uncles and brothers highly involved in family life, and people who were quite isolated from family or did not wish to have children. There were many people in relationships who had never married, but there were also people who were dating, people in polyamorous relationships, people who were single, people who were divorced. There were married men in long-term relationships who had been with their wives since before their transition, along with gay men and pansexuals, and people who had experienced a variety of relations and defied generic labels. Whilst this study showed themes and commonalities in the Australian context, it is important to remember that all FtM transgender people are individuals and should not be stereotyped.

Recommendations

The issues and implications emerging from this research covered a range of fields, and involved a number of stakeholders from governments through to service workers and everyday citizens. Our recommendations include consideration of public safety and social supports, documentation, education policy, employment policy, health and medical policy, gender identity clinics, mental health services, further research and advocacy.

Public Safety and Social Supports

There needs to be more campaigns against both homophobia and transphobia on the street, and the ways people can assist or numbers people can contact in the event of such crises. Both these types of discrimination impact gender non-conforming people in particular. Advocacy about trans-identity is necessary in order for social networks to be more accepting, understanding and non-judgemental of difference (including queer organisations, churches, choirs and other social structures the participants mentioned). Emergency crisis bedding for people who experience negative responses when coming out as transgender to family or partners is important; some participants had experienced violent reactions from family.

The respondents also suggested the need for mandatory gender diversity awareness training for government body staff, involving transgender people in activisms at educational institutions so they can advocate for their needs directly to large groups of people, and having local queer youth workers as support for people across Australia. To enhance the social representation and connectivity of FtM transgender people particularly, participants encouraged the development of local "boys groups" to allow people to make trans* friends, and support groups for partners, as well as equal representation of transgender people at the gay and lesbian Mardi Gras parades and events.

Documentation

The national *Guidelines on the Recognition of Sex and Gender* are to be implemented within three years (Australian Government 2013). We applaud the introduction of more streamlined guidelines, and the 2013 intervention of then Federal Health Minister Tanya Plibersek into Medicare's conditions which opened up the requirements around transition in an effort towards equity. We urge all government offices (including Centrelink offices), Medicare offices, post offices, banks, educational institutions, legal offices, real estate agents, social services and other places where documentation is required (featuring name and sex) to familiarise staff with the guidelines and to help make these processes consistent. This includes video stores, gyms, libraries and other such sites which issue identification cards; and shops which issue cards based on points systems.

National anti-discrimination law now makes discriminatory treatment of transgender people unlawful, and it is important to be aware of the requirements but also the ways in which they should be applied. Sensitivity training around these processes are recommended, so that staff handle these transitions with tact, discretion and professionalism. It is important that staff realise the vulnerable position people are in when requesting documentation changes. Thus, 'outing' their transgender status—regardless of whether or not the requirements have been met—is in appropriate. It is not a crime to attempt to change one's documents as relevant. The applicant should be treated with respect. They should be given the information they need to pursue the change.

It is particularly important for lawyers and gender support workers to familiarise themselves with the new documentation guidelines. This will enable them to better advocate for this group in cases where documentation changes are more difficult and require further action. Some transgender individuals may find the process particularly distressful and may need support.

Education Policy

Australia needs a national education policy on GLBTIQ issues, which includes guidelines around combatting transphobia and the practical issues of supporting transgender people's needs in education. This should be framed as a rolling out of the new federal anti-discrimination protections around gender identity in education. This policy should include information on the need for state and school level protective policies which research has correlated with a reduction in school violence, self-harm and suicide risk for GLBTIQ students. The policy should also require schools to provide information through wellbeing units and sex education (or other areas as they see fit) on GLBTIQ identity and rights. Guidelines should also cover the provision of transgender-friendly counselling or referrals, unisex or more flexible access to uniforms or bathrooms, management plans in which the student and their advocate are included, and professional attitudes. This policy—and any existing state and school level policies—needs to be properly launched and promoted to school leaders.

GLBTIQ issues should be included in sex education and health in the forthcoming *Australian National Curriculum*; there was no excuse for its removal in the most recent draft and indeed we believe that in light of new laws on equitable education services, this kind of oversight in the field of sex education is highly problematic. Transgender youth deserve equitable access to education and to relevant sex education information consistent with international human rights provisions, sex education policy and education for all statements (UNESCO 2009, 2011; United Nations 2012).

All educational institutions (universities, schools, TAFEs and other education centres) should provide equity training that includes coverage of transgender issues for all their staff and students (administration through to teachers and counsellors). It is important for teacher education degrees and diplomas, as well as training for psychologists and counsellors, to include basic coverage of these issues within at least one core required unit of study (preferably engaged in prior to practicum units). Relying on transgender staff to deal with transphobia against students puts them in an untenable position (Harris and Jones 2014; Jones et al. 2014); this is the work of *all* education staff.

Displays outside staffrooms and counsellors' offices that show support for gender questioning youth in schools are particularly important, and can be used as a means to offer information and supports (including Kids Helpline and Lifeline contacts). These displays send a welcoming message without requiring the child to "come out" or makes decisions about their identity in order to simply access support. The emphasis in schools should be on letting kids be themselves around gender (regardless of its expression), so that completing their education, not feeling distressed about their gender identity, can be their focus in such environments.

Employment Policy

Workplace Equity training should include transphobia and guidelines for dealing with transgender issues in the workplace regardless of whether or not a space is "perceived" to have FtM transgender (or any transgender) employees. It should incorporate mention of the national and state protections around gender identity relevant to the work site's location.

Unions could consider a particular targeting of male environments for anti-transphobia campaigns centred on the new national anti-discrimination law protections around gender identity and expression, with such cultures highlighted for potentially supporting transphobic and homophobic language in the workplace. Transgender people should not feel restricted to working in particular fields (creative arts, care), but must be enabled to pursue careers best fitting their skills and interests like any Australian (in the true spirit of equity).

Leadership from supervisors, management and equity officers is necessary to combat transphobia in the general culture of an organisation. This is also important during recruitment and promotion, and during any individual staff member's transitions or affirmations of their gender identity. We recommend working with any individual staff member who does come forward as transgender or transitioning, to determine their needs around medical concerns and use of facilities, and discretely ensure other staff use the employee's preferred pronouns and forms of address.

Health and Medical Policy

There is a need to ensure young people, genderqueer people and people in rural areas are better catered to. Young people and genderqueer people appeared to know of more people in their own groups who had experienced difficulties with getting doctors/psychologists' supports for hormone therapy for example, which did place the groups at higher risk of seeking to use other people's prescriptions or considering buying unapproved hormones online. These would obviously be dangerous moves and need to be circumvented through accessible services.

People in rural areas needed more transgender-friendly health and mental health services and supports, and clearly greater training in gender identity issues must become standard across health qualifications. However in the meantime, it might be possible for counsellors or other providers to consider using online means of offering access to these people. Perhaps offering sessions via Skype, telephone or online forums sometimes so that other in-person sessions can be saved-up for, whilst training is rolled out, could meet needs in the interim.

Some participants did not disclose their transgender identity to their health-care providers, so posters/displays showing that transgender people are welcome should be used to communicate that it is safe to disclose such information. Information on gender identity should be made available to people without requiring them to "come out" as gender questioning to obtain it (through a pamphlet stand for example).

Health and medical training must include coverage of gender identity issues, and GLBTIQ/transgender identities, in early core units of study. For existing staff and services, there should be sensitivity training around using the pronouns a patient prefers and treating a patient's gender questioning and sense of self with respect. Gender diversity should not be treated with ridicule, disbelief or resistance. Health-care services should ask patients their preferred name and pronouns on application forms, and then train staff to follow up on and use these words. Respondents greatly valued health-care providers who educated themselves on transgender issues, were friendly, treated them in accordance with their gender identity and went above and beyond to help them get the assistance from other services that they required.

Gender Identity Clinics, Experts and Services

There is a strong need for appropriate gender clinics and appropriate services in many Australian states (for example Queensland). This country needs more gender identity experts. It also needs more training in gender identity issues for doctors, counsellors, psychiatrists, surgeons, and a range of other medical and health practitioners who may engage with FtM transgender Australians on various gender affirmation journeys (which may or may not include medical treatments). There is an urgent need for more specialists also in surgical practices like phalloplasty and related bottom surgeries for FtM people.

There needs to be consistent training requirements across all states and territories, a regular process of auditing and review to check clinics and doctors are in compliance—and moreover, to ensure good clinics are being supported in their good practice with the funds and staff they need to continue. Research-based standards of care for transgender people need to developed, disseminated and applied.

Accreditation processes should be publicly visible; the training and some information about the prior work achievements of practitioners and experts should be displayed in their offices or made accessible for patients considering using their services. We need to shift the power dynamic so that potential patients have greater choice and more of a voice, rather than have so few options that they must "put up with" bad practice in the hope of being able to one day transition or access treatments they simply cannot get elsewhere.

Mental Health Services

There need to be more mental health services which specialise in gender identity issues, and greater access to these services from a range of locations (perhaps through well-considered online and telephone contact options). Services should be able to respond to the need for diagnoses around GID, paperwork, long-term issues (particularly depression and anxiety), understanding gender identity and resilience, dealing with social relationships and contexts, and moments of crises. All mental health providers must be trained in GLBTIQ issues and particularly transgender peoples' needs—for many transgender people accessing mental health services is not optional (either in relation to transitions or other needs). For this reason, overly expensive psychiatry fees should be reconsidered where the treatment is urgent and necessary in relation to a transition or crises. Service-providers need to be aware of the high rates of self-harm and suicide in this group, and should offer training in coping skills during difficult periods. They should particularly seek to treat patients/clients' own personal issues in accepting and expressing their gender identity, which were a key factor in wellbeing risks. There should be greater regulation of standards in psychology and psychiatry on transgender issues, particularly around how much time is spent in diagnoses of GID. Providers should make efforts to take an interest in patients/clients, and to be non-judgemental.

Sexual Health Resources

Whilst some participants found their transitions and gender affirmations did not impact their relationships or sexual lives much, or become more wary of sexual interactions, other participants appeared to enter a period of sexual awakening after starting testosterone, increasing their libido and becoming more comfortable with their bodies. Many became more interested in a range of experimentations, sexual options and partners. Many assumed that they were making safe choices, regardless of the fact that they used no protection for receiving vaginal or anal penetrative sex with men—it was unclear the extent to which they had been advised or not about reproductive risks and STI risks, and whether the information was specific to their needs as FtM transgender people and their relationship contexts etc. Because use of protections and choices in sexual practices were so varied, and impacted by transitions, some sexual health resources specific to FtM Australians are needed. Information on the precise impacts of hormones on the reproductive system "as a form of protection" (or not) needs to be disseminated, and information on susceptibilities to various STIs and various protections would also be useful. As FtM people are often required to see psychologists and doctors as part of gender affirmation processes, early appointments could provide health practitioners with key opportunities to pass on sexual health information.

Further Research

Areas for further investigation that emerged from this study include those identified by both the researchers, and the participants themselves. The forum was specifically designed to encourage unforeseen themes to emerge, and to also encourage participants to take more control of the direction of the research (commenting on questions or offering ideas). This is because it is important to challenge the normative dynamic of research wherein transgender people historically have had little control over how they are represented. Whilst some of the themes suggested by participants were then explored during this project as they arose, others still remained less of a feature of the study (either because they were suggested later on in the life of the forum, or overlooked by other participants in the forum). Family life—particularly areas such as having children, being parents, coming out to children (whether as a father/parent, uncle/relative or otherwise) was a central area of interest. We explored parenting to some degree through the discussion boards but had not asked quantitative questions on the topic within our survey. We encourage future researchers to generate such statistical data. It could also be useful to pitch research towards developing and trialling resources for transgender parents.

Research into "what works" to help FtM people come to terms with their personal issues with their gender identity (given how often these issues were cited as a primary factor in self-harm and suicide attempts) is an imperative, alongside research into developing best-practice standards for health services, and research into the implementation rate of new policy on documentation. Another possibility is research into how online platforms can be used to meet interstate health service lacks for transgender people. Other suggestions for future research from the participants themselves included the need for documentary-style inquiries which could be televised, combining interviews and observation during key life moments. This was an interesting idea that suggested that new media could be incorporated to achieve both visibility and data. One participant suggested that research on how FtM people experience father-son relationships as a self-made son could be useful in understanding difficulties around gaining male role models during transition. Some of the participants planned to engage in their own research projects in the field in the future, and we strongly encourage them to do so. Research on FtM transgender issues by FtM transgender people is rare and will greatly enhance the field by potentially helping it move further away from pathologising tropes.

Future Advocacy

The Sex Discrimination Amendment (Sexual Orientation, Gender Identity and Intersex Status) Act 2013 (Cth) (SDA Amendment Act) means complaints about discrimination on the basis of gender identity can now be made directly to the Australian Human Rights Commission. A broader definition of gender identity is being used in the SDA Amendment Act than has been used at the state-level, so whereas in some states and territories the protections offered in law were around discrimination against one's gender history, or transsexual status for example (with a presumption of transition and binary sex), here gender identity is also being used in terms of gender-related identity, appearance or mannerisms or other gender-related characteristics.

How gender is expressed/presented is also covered, with greater recognition that a person's gender identity may be an identity other than male or female… so there is more coverage now for genderqueer expression, for people who don't follow strict notions of transition, for someone who is not strictly defining as male but still wants to wear the so-called "men's uniform" at work rather than an allocated skirt. A much broader spectrum of people are protected from a broader range of potential discrimination on the basis of gender identity. Advocates of transgender rights are encouraged to disseminate information about these new protections, and the complaints processes through the Australian Human Rights Commission, through their networks. They are also encouraged to promote information about the newly released *Guidelines on the Recognition of Sex and Gender* (Australian Government 2013), the changes to Medicare and so on so that FtM Australians can make use of these new provisions.

Advocates can promote awareness of the protections through developing national training/equity inductions on these issues that can be used in various sectors. They can encourage the insertion of information about the new laws in the national curriculum, the development of national sector policies citing the law/ guidelines (in education, health, and so on), and respond to the likely cases of national impact that will arise out of the national law changes. Interstate collaborations for advice, training and so on will now have a stronger basis as contexts will become more aligned. Resources (books, posters, pamphlets) can be made with a national, rather than just a state, readership/audience in mind.

This study has shown that many Transgender FtM people feel isolated because of the state or territory they live in—it will now be entirely possible for FtM support groups in one state to help an individual deal with a discrimination case in another, and advocates (and federal funding bodies) should recognise this opportunity and help make their organisations more accessible for such work.

Conclusion

It has been an honour to do this study, and at times a very humbling learning experience. We dedicate this book to FtM transgender Australians—the men, the boys, and the transgender and genderqueer people who form this rich and diverse community in Australia. We admire and thank them for their candidness, insights and advice. We appreciated their sense of humour. We encourage all stakeholders to act on these recommendations in support for their future, as Australia moves into a new period of reform on transgender issues and equality for all people regardless of their gender identity. We encourage Australians to embrace our FtM trangender community members.

Appendix A
The Survey Questionnaire

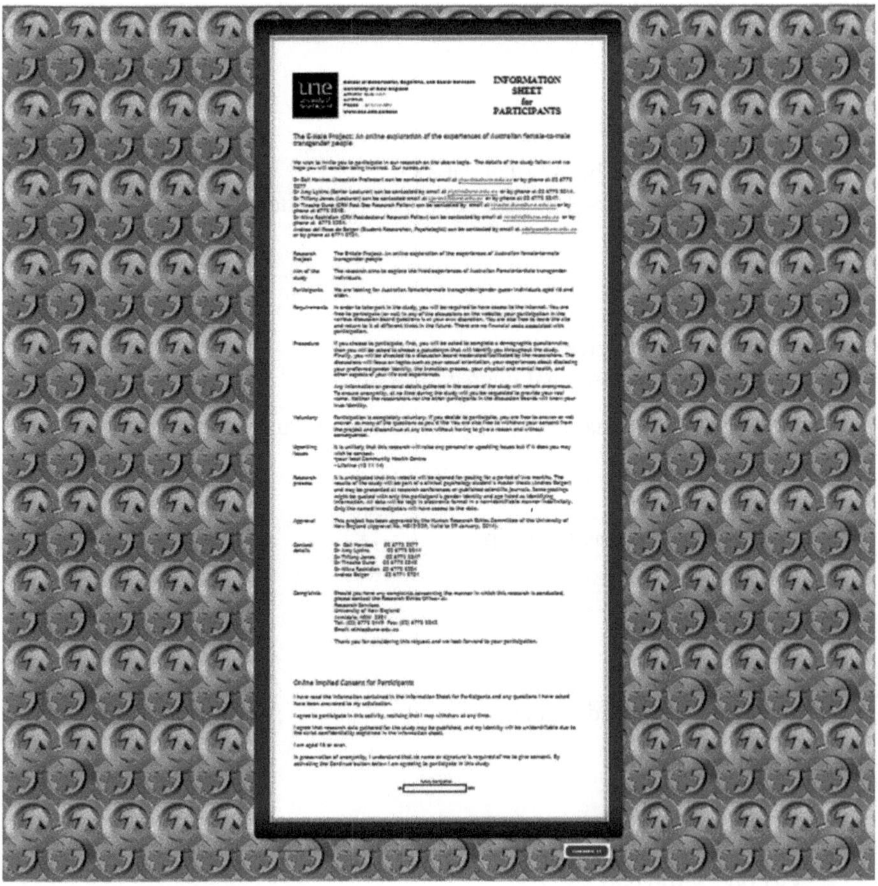

INFORMATION
SHEET
for
PARTICIPANTS

T. Jones et al., *Female-to-Male (FtM) Transgender People's Experiences in Australia*, SpringerBriefs in Sociology, DOI 10.1007/978-3-319-13829-9

Survey Questions

Postcode

Age

1. What of the following best describes the **gender role/gender identity** you identify with? (mandatory)
    a. Male
    b. Female
    c. Transsexual male
    d. FtM transgender
    e. Genderqueer
    f. Other
2. What is your assigned gender on your birth certificate? (mandatory)
    a. Male
    b. Female
    c. Intersex
3. What is your date of birth? (mandatory)
4. What is the highest level of education you have attained so far?
    a. Primary
    b. Secondary
    c. TAFE
    d. Undergraduate degree
    e. Postgraduate/professional degree.
5. Tick all the options that apply to your current circumstances:
    a. I am at school
    b. I am at TAFE
    c. I am doing an apprenticeship
    d. I am at University
    e. I work full-time
    f. I work part-time
    g. I am unemployed
6. What is your estimated annual income?
    a. Less than $20,000
    b. $20,000–$40,000
    c. $41,000–$60,000
    d. $61,000–$80,000
    e. $81,000–$100,000
    f. $101,000+
7. What is your country of origin?
8. What is your ethnicity?

9. Do you identify with a specific religious denomination?

   a. Christianity
   b. Judaism
   c. Hinduism
   d. Islam
   e. Buddhism
   f. Atheist/None
   g. Agnostic/Undecided
   h. Other (Specify ____)

10. What is your postal code?
11. What is your current relationship status?

    a. Single and not dating
    b. Single and dating
    c. In a monogamous relationship
    d. In a non-monogamous (open) relationship
    e. In a polyamorous (multiple people) relationship

12. What is your legal marital status right now? Tick all the items that apply to you.

    a. Never married
    b. Separated
    c. Divorced
    d. Widowed
    e. De facto
    f. Married

13. What are your current living arrangements? I live…

    a. With family
    b. On my own
    c. With my partner
    d. With friends
    e. In a Refuge
    f. At College
    g. I couch surf
    h. On the Street/car
    i. Other (specify)

14. Do you identify as a person with a disability? If so, please specify.

Physical Health

15. How would you describe your physical health in the last 12 months?

    a. Very bad
    b. Bad
    c. Neither good nor bad

d. Good
e. Very good

Mental Health

16. In the last 12 months, have you received any of these mental health diagnoses?

a. Depression
b. Adjustment Disorder
c. Anxiety
d. Post-Traumatic Stress Disorder
e. Obsessive Compulsive Disorder
f. Schizophrenia
g. Borderline Personality Disorder
h. Body Dysmorphic Disorder
i. Other

17. Do you use

	Daily?	Weekly?	Fortnightly?	Monthly?	Occasionally?	Never?
Alcohol						
Cigarettes						
Marijuana						
Amphetamines						
Cocaine						
Ectasy						
Inhalants						
Hallucinogens						
Sedatives						
Non-prescribed stimulants						
Heroin						

18. Have you ever **self-harmed** (or had thoughts about, plans towards causing yourself physical pain)?
Was this related to (tick any/all that apply):

- Experiences of transphobia from other people/institutions
- Your personal issues with your gender identity/being trans*
- Other reasons

19. Have you ever experienced **suicidal ideation** (thoughts about, plans towards suicide)?
Were these thoughts related to (tick any/all that apply):

- Experiences of transphobia from other people/institutions
- Your personal issues with your gender identity/being trans*
- Other reasons

20. Have you ever **attempted suicide**?
Were your actions related to (tick any/all that apply):

- Experiences of transphobia from other people/institutions
- Your personal issues with your gender identity/being trans*
- Other reasons

21. How would you describe your level of satisfaction with

	Very dissatisfied	Dissatisfied	Neutral	Satisfied	Very satisfied
Your life in general?					
Your social life?					
Your romantic life?					
Your sexual life?					
Your physical health?					
Your job/studies?					

Transitioning

22. Have you ever had physical interventions to make your body appear more masculine?

   a. Yes
   b. No

23. If yes, what types of physical modifications have you gone through? Tick the options that apply to you:

   a. Binding
   b. Packing
   c. Wearing a prosthetic penis
   d. Taking puberty blockers
   e. Taking hormones
   f. Mastectomy
   g. Chest surgery
   h. Genital surgery
   i. Other… (please specify)

24. Do you intend to have additional physical modifications?

   a. Yes. Please specify
   b. No

25. How satisfied are you with the results?

    a. Very satisfied
    b. Satisfied
    c. Neutral
    d. Dissatisfied
    e. Very dissatisfied

26. Has it made a difference to your life and the way you feel?

    a. Yes
    b. No

27. Have you sought surgical treatments or medications overseas due to financial or other reasons?

    a. Yes
    b. No

28. Because of restrictions on medical/surgical provisions or because you don't fit the category of FtM used in Australia or for age reasons, have you been forced to break the law or engage in black-market treatments, or use unapproved treatments or someone else's prescription?

    a. Yes
    b. No

Body Appearance

29. How would you rate your current physical appearance along this scale?

    a. Feminine
    b. Neutral
    c. Masculine

Sexuality

30. Who are you attracted to?

    a. Only to people of my own sex
    b. People of both sexes
    c. People of the opposite sex
    d. It changes
    e. I am not sure

31. How did you find out about the project?

    a. Webpage (please name)
    b. Friend
    c. Other (please identify)

Appendix B
The Forum Questionnaire

E-males Study Discussion Board

Welcome to the *E-males* Project! Thank you for your interest in participating in this study; we are looking forward to hearing about your experiences and opinions on a variety of topics (e.g., gender identity, coming out, experiences with health and mental healthcare, etc.). You can find the topics of interest in the hyperlinks listed above. Please feel free to comment on as many of these topics as you wish. Please remember to SAVE this URL so that you can return to the page if you'd like to add more at a later time. Please also remember to always use the same pseudonym so that we can tie your remarks on these pages with your demographic data.

In the interest of maintaining your anonymity, please do not reveal any personally identifying information (i.e., your name) on these pages. This research is being conducted to benefit the trans community, and as such we ask that all participants are respectful to members of this community and of their need for confidentiality. Please therefore be respectful to other participants, and do not harass people you believe you may know to disclose either their 'real-world' or their 'forum' identity, within or beyond the forum. We thank you very much for your participation and look forward to hearing from you.

You may use a unique number as your pseudonym, instead of letters/a name, for added anonymity, if you choose.

Gender Identity

1. How do you prefer to identify yourself (e.g., male, female, transgender FtM, Genderqueer, other)?
2. How do you define your gender identity and how would you describe it?
3. About how old were you when you first became aware that your gender identity did not match your body or physical appearance? What was that like?

Coming Out

1. How would you describe your current openness about your gender identity?
2. Can you explain why you have chosen to open up, or why you have chosen not to open up?

T. Jones et al., *Female-to-Male (FtM) Transgender People's Experiences in Australia*, SpringerBriefs in Sociology, DOI 10.1007/978-3-319-13829-9

3. What impact has your disclosure or silence had on your life?
4. Who, specifically, have you disclosed your gender identity/status/history to and how did they treat your disclosure at the time.
5. Has anyone changed their treatment of you over time (from supportive to unsupportive or vice versa)?

Transitioning and impact on wellbeing

1. Have you ever had physical interventions to make your body appear more masculine? If yes, what types?
2. How much money have you invested in this process so far?
3. How satisfied are you with the results?
4. Has it made a difference to your life and the way you feel?
5. Do you intend to do more? Why or why not?
6. Have you sought surgical treatments or medications overseas due to financial or other reasons?
7. Have you been forced to break the law or engage in black-market treatments, or use unapproved treatments or someone else's prescription because of restrictions on medical/surgical provisions? Please tell us about this.

Sexuality

1. Who are you attracted to?
   Are you attracted more to
   - femininity,
   - masculinity,
   - both,
   - other gender expressions,
   - all gender expressions,
   - Or is your attraction to gender variable or not important for you?
2. How do you define your sexual orientation? (heterosexual, gay, pansexual…?)
3. Can you discuss your previous and/or current sexual relationships?
4. How has being transgender/genderqueer impacted on your sexual life?
5. This question is to help us provide information and debunk myths about trans* sexualities for trans* people and towards sexual health services provisions. However, you do not need to answer if you do not feel comfortable. What sexual acts would you feel comfortable engaging in, given the right circumstances/partner?

- none,
- kissing,
- performing oral sex,
- receiving oral sex,
- performing penetrative sex through the front hole (vaginal)
- receiving penetrative sex through the front hole (vaginal)
- performing penetrative sex anal,

- receiving penetrative sex anal,
- wearing a strap on,
- anything,
- other

6. What kind of protection against STDs/pregnancy do you use (oral contraception, glove, condom, dental dam, none etc.)

Life Satisfaction

1. How do you feel life is going generally? What are the best areas of your life? Are there elements you wish you could change about it?
2. How would you describe your level of satisfaction with who you are?
3. How would you describe your level of satisfaction with your sexual life?

General wellbeing and quality of life

1. How would you describe your family relationships?
2. How would you describe your social relationships?
3. How would you describe your romantic relationships?

Mental health

1. How would you describe your mental health? Do you feel happy? Do you struggle with mental health issues? If so, why do you think these issues have arisen?

Gender identity clinics

1. How much interaction have you had with gender identity clinics? What have these experiences been like?

Health care

1. What has your experience with heath service-providers been like so far?
2. Do you think they have an understanding of transgender people?
3. Can you tell us about a good experience and a bad experience you have had?
4. What would you change or add to these services?

Mental health services

1. What types of mental health services have you accessed and why?
2. What were your experiences with these services?

Social inclusion

1. Have you ever been discriminated on the basis of your gender identity? Tell us about your experience.
2. How has this affected you?

Education

1. Did/does your school have an anti-bullying policy that protected trans* people?
2. Did/does your school provide any information to students about trans* identities or issues (in sex education, science or any other subject)?

3. Did/does your school have a trans* friendly counsellor?
4. Did/does your school have unisex uniform options (outfits someone of any sex/ gender identity could wear)?
5. Did/does your school have unisex toilet options (toilets someone of any sex/ gender identity could use)?
6. What is/was your school's attitude towards diverse gender identities?
7. Is/Was it possible for you to express your gender identity at school? How, how not?
8. What kind of things would improve or would have improved your experience in the school system?

Employment opportunities

1. Has your gender identity ever become an obstacle for your career or employment aspirations? Please tell us about this.

Supports and community involvement

1. Are you actively engaged in activism for the rights of transgender people?
2. Have you ever received support from a transgender group?
3. Who are your supports?
4. What would you like to see in terms of trans* community activism, supports or events?

Legal issues

1. Have you tried to amend documentation to reflect your current gender identity? If "Yes", what was the experience like? Why is this important to you?
2. Have you had any difficulties around getting your documentation changed that you would like to share with us?

Positive experiences

1. Tell us about a positive story about experiences of support, resilience or empowerment in your life.

Other

1. If there is a topic that is important to you related to FtM or broader trans* issues that we have overlooked, please name that topic here and tell us about it.
2. Please let us know any specific question researchers should explore in future projects?

Family

1. Do you have children? or would you like to have children?
2. How do you explain your gender identity and process of transformation to them or other members of your family?
3. What is their reaction to your gender identity?

I think that for the most part I am happy. I try not to allow myself to focus on the belief that "I will be happier when..." (Insert next stage of medical transition) this can cause negative thinking that clouds the positive forward movement. Medical transition is a long process and life happens every day (Maddox, male/ftm/transman, 21 years).

I think one of the best experiences I had (besides getting married and being there at the birth of my child)... was when a gay man asked me out. I felt like, well if he couldn't tell. I have nothing to worry about! I Thanked him for the offer, it was flattering (more than he will ever know), but I told him I am not interested in men (doc79, male, 33 years).

I would also never use a prescription or medication prescribed or belonging to anyone else, maybe it's because I'm older, maybe it's because I know better, maybe it's because of some other reason I can't remember or a combination of any or all, nonetheless I would never do it (zbdsm, male, 57 years).

Other thing I would like to see is better (and compulsory) inclusion of trans and intersex people our needs and specific health and cultural sensitivity issues in the medical school curriculum (rather than a one sentence brush-off under Psychiatry) and in allied health curriculum as well. At present there is limited coverage from biased people who aren't themselves part of the trans* and gender diverse community, and it's not compulsory to attend the lectures (and/or they are not assessed). Can't improve awareness and knowledge of health professionals without education from the earliest stages of training process! Specialists, GPs and allied health all need awareness* (Garfield, male/man of trans heritage/PDQ—pretty damn queer, 31 years).

T. Jones et al., *Female-to-Male (FtM) Transgender People's Experiences in Australia*, SpringerBriefs in Sociology, DOI 10.1007/978-3-319-13829-9

Glossary

This glossary has been compiled in relation to Female-to-Male Transgender issues, so where a term (such as chest surgery) might have different meanings in different contexts, here the meaning in relation to Female-to-Male Transgender issues is privileged. Some of the definitions first featured in previous publications (Jones 2012b*; Jones and Hillier* 2012). *We are aware sometimes terms will be used by people in different ways and some are contested, but wanted to provide people with a starting point for understanding such diversities as they emerged in the research.*

Androgynous Can mean having both masculine and feminine characteristics, or having neither specifically masculine nor feminine characteristics. Some people who are androgynous may identify as genderqueer, trans or androgynous

Bilateral salpingo-oophorectomy/BSO The removal of both ovaries and fallopian tubes

Binder/Binding Binding involves flattening/de-emphasising one's chest tissues using a binder. Binders can range from a generic piece of loose cloth/rag tied or wrapped around the chest and held in place with a clip or fasten, through to specially designed and commercially available materials, vests, compression tops or singlets. Binding should not involve Ace bandages or duct tape, and should not be engaged in for more than 8–12 h at a time for health reasons

Bisexual or Bi Refers to people whose sexual and romantic feelings are for both men and women, and who identify with these feelings. Many people may engage in bisexual behaviours but not identify as bisexual. See also: pansexual or omnisexual

Blockers See puberty blockers

Bottom Surgery Can involve for example sterilisation, hysterectomy, bilateral salpingo-oophorectomy/BSO, and/or genital reconstructive procedures/GRT (metoidioplasty—enlarging the clitoris with androgenic hormones or free tissue grafts from the arm, the thigh or belly; and/or phalloplasty—insertion of an erectile prosthetic; and/or rerouting the urethra through the phallus to allow urination/scrotum, insertion of prosthetic testicles etc)

T. Jones et al., *Female-to-Male (FtM) Transgender People's Experiences in Australia*, SpringerBriefs in Sociology, DOI 10.1007/978-3-319-13829-9

Cisgendered Refers to people whose sense of gender and/or sex matches the sex they were assigned at birth. Cisgender is the antonym of transgender and is used to label those whose gender is not trans

Chest Surgery Can involve reduction (the surgical reduction in size/amount of the chest tissue), mastectomy (surgical removal of one or both breasts/chest tissue, partially or completely), chest contouring/reconstruction (giving the chest a male aesthetic through implants, sculpturing of tissue, tattooing etc.) or related surgeries

Cis/cisgender/cissexual Describes gender identity where an individual's self-perception of their gender matches the sex they were assigned at birth. For example, a cis male was assigned male at birth, and this label fits his gender identity

Cisgender privilege Advantages that individuals who identify as the gender they were assigned at birth experience

Cissexism Discrimination based on the assumption that transgender people are inferior to, or less authentic than, cisgender people

Depo-Provera/depot medroxyprogesterone acetate/DMPA Can be used to reduce or eliminate menses/menstruation, generally injected every three months (just as it is used for contraception)

FtM/F-M/F2M See Transgender FtM

Gay People whose sexual and romantic feelings are primarily for the same sex and who identify primarily with those feelings. In Australia, both men and women identify as gay, however it often refers mainly to homosexual men

Gender Identity The gender-related identity, appearance or mannerisms or other gender-related characteristics of an individual (whether by way of medical intervention or not, socialisation or alternative expression), with or without regard to the individual's designated sex at birth, and includes transsexualism and transgenderism

Genderqueer Can be used as an umbrella term similar to Transgender but commonly refers to people who are not transsexual, but do not comply with their traditional gender expectations through their dress, hair, mannerisms, appearance and values

GLBTIQ Gay, lesbian, bisexual, transgender, intersex and otherwise questioning (people)

Hormone Therapy/Hormone Replacement Therapy/HRT For transgender and transsexual people this form of treatment introduces hormones associated with the gender that the patient identifies with (e.g. testosterone for FtM transgender individuals). The treatment causes the development of secondary sex characteristics, although impacts vary (e.g. this can include increased hair growth on face and body, lowered voice, more masculine appearance in terms of facial features and muscle/fat distributions on the body, enlargement of the clitoris, changes in energy levels/mood/appetite, changes in emotional experience, male pattern baldness in some individuals and so on). Testosterone may be delivered via injections, transdermal applications (patches, creams, gels), subcutaneous pellets (inserted under the skin every few months), orally (as tablets), or sub-lingual/buccal form (absorbed through the mouth mucus rather than 'eaten' as such). Androgens, pro-hormones or supplements also might or might not be part of a treatment plan

Homophobia An individual's or society's misunderstanding, fear, ignorance of, or prejudice against gay, lesbian and/or bisexual people

Homosexual People whose sexual and romantic feelings are primarily for the same sex and who identify primarily with those feelings. People who feel this way often identify as gay or lesbian

Hysterectomy Surgical removal of the uterus

Intersex status The status of having physical, hormonal or genetic features that are—(a) neither wholly female nor wholly male or (b) a combination of female and male or (c) neither female nor male

Gender Dysphoria A medical diagnosis related to transgender people in the DSM-V, which refers to extreme discontent with the assigned sex allocated to an individual at birth

Gender Identity Disorder/GID A medical diagnosis for transgender people used in the DSM-IV and since replaced with gender dysphoria (which is seen as less stigmatising)

Genital reconstructive procedures/GRT Procedures which construct a phallus, using either the clitoris, which is enlarged by androgenic hormones (metoidioplasty) or free tissue grafts from the arm, the thigh or belly and an erectile prosthetic (phalloplasty). The urethra can be rerouted through the phallus to allow urination through the reconstructed penis. The labia majora can be united to form a scrotum, prosthetic testicles can be inserted

Lesbian Women whose sexual and romantic feelings are primarily for other women and who identify with those feelings

Mastectomy The medical term for the surgical removal of one or both breasts, partially or completely

Metoidioplasty The medical term for the enlarging of the clitoris with androgenic hormones or free tissue grafts from the arm, the thigh or belly

MtF/M-F/M2F See Transgender MtF

Packing Wearing padding or a phallic object (can be a specially designed 'packer'/phallus) in one's pants or underwear

Pansexual or Omnisexual Refers to people whose sexual and romantic feelings are for all genders; this rejects the gender binary of male/female and asserts that there are more than two genders or gender identities. These are inclusive terms that consider the gender diverse community

Phalloplasty The medical term for surgical procedures in which an erectile prosthetic is inserted as part of genital reconstruction

Prosthetic A medical term for an artificial device that replaces a body part that is missing

Puberty Blockers Non-testosterone based hormone treatment (GnRH agonists) used to suspend the advance of sex steroid induced and thus block pubertal changes (and secondary sex characteristics) from occurring/developing further for a period of time. No changes in terms of transition to the desired sex/gender identity occur; this measure is generally understood to be preparation for transitions/decisions around transitions, rather than a transition process itself

Queer Queer is an umbrella term used to refer to the LGBT community. Some people in the GLBTIQ community prefer not to use this term as the history of the word has negative connotations. These days, the term has been embraced and is more about pride, inclusivity and sometimes even a kind of political subversiveness (a resistance to "normative" identity)

Sex The physiological make-up of a person. It is commonly expressed as a binary and used to divide people into males and females. However, in reality, sex is a complex relationship of genetic, hormonal, morphological, biochemical, and anatomical differences. These various differences impact both the physiology of the body and the sexual differentiation of the brain. Although everyone is assigned a sex at birth, researchers argue that approximately 2–4 % of the population are intersexed and do not fit easily into a dimorphic division of two sexes that are "opposite"

Sexual Orientation The direction of one's sexual and romantic attractions and interests toward members of the same, opposite or both sexes, or all genders. Similar to 'Sexual Preference'

Strap on A dildo/external prosthesis strapped on to the outside of the body/worn with a harness, which may be used in sex, but is sometimes used for packing (to fill out clothing for example)

'T'/Testosterone See Hormone Therapy

Trans/Transgender A broad umbrella term, including people/a person who identifies as a sex different to the one assigned at birth and who may choose to undergo sex affirmation/reassignment surgery(ies). Describes a broad range of non-conforming gender identities and/or behaviours

Transsexual/TS People/a person who identifies as a sex different to the one assigned at birth and who may choose to undergo sex affirmation/reassignment surgery(ies). For example, a man who was assigned female sex at birth, and has subsequently corrected this issue through transition processes to address the physical issues of TS

Transition/Transitioning Refers to the process (either past current or future) of personally, socially, physically and/or legally changing ones' gender presentation/sex to some extent (whether slightly through to wholly). This process can involve changing how one refers to/sees themselves, changing the way one dresses or presents themselves (hairstyle and so forth), changing how one is referred to/seen by others (pronouns like his/her, he/she/they/ze), and/or changing one's social role or role in relationships if relevant. It might also involve changing one's body through hormonal therapies/cosmetic procedures/a range of surgeries, and/or changing the way one is identified by sex on legal or reporting documents (birth certificate, passport, license, and/or other records like academic records)

Transgender FtM A person who was born as female or intersex (or otherwise not strictly male) who identifies as a sex different to the one assigned at birth (as male, a transman or genderqueer for example) and who may choose to undergo sex affirmation/reassignment surgery(ies). Describes a broad range of non-conforming gender identities and/or behaviours, and we use the term in a broad sense in this study to include people who identify from precisely to broadly with this category

Transgender MtF A person who was born as male or intersex (or otherwise not strictly female) who identifies as a sex different to the one assigned at birth (as female, a transwoman or genderqueer) and who may choose to undergo sex affirmation/reassignment surgery(ies). Describes a broad range of non-conforming gender identities and/or behaviours

Transphobia An individual's or society's misunderstanding, fear, ignorance of, or prejudice against transgender people

References

ACT Government. (2007a). *Countering bullying, harassment and violence in ACT public schools. Canberra: ACT department of education and training*. Retrieved from http://www.det.act.gov.au/publications_and_policies/policy_a-z.

ACT Government. (2007b). *Countering sexual harassment in public schools. Canberra: ACT department of education and training*. Retrieved from http://www.det.act.gov.au/publications_and_policies/policy_a-z.

ACT Government. (2007c). *Equity and diversity plan 2007–2009. Canberra: ACT department of education and training*. Retrieved from http://www.det.act.gov.au/publications_and_policies/policy_a-z.

Anti-Discrimination Act 1991. (2010). *QLD parliamentary counsel, reprint no. 9B congressional record*

Anti-Discrimination Act 1997. (2010). *NSW parliamentary counsel, 48 congressional record.*

Anti-Discrimination Act 1992. (2010). *NT department of justice, REPA027 congressional record*

Anti-Discrimination Act 1991. (2010). *ACT parliamentary counsel, 35 Congressional Record.*

Australian Bureau of Statistics. (2012a). *1301.0—Year book Australia: Educational attainment*. Retrieved from http://www.abs.gov.au/ausstats/abs@.nsf/Lookup/bySubject/1301.0 ~ 2012 ~ MainFeatures ~ Educationalattainment ~ 110.

Australia, O. I. I. (2012). *Intersex for allies*. Melbourne: OII Australia.

Australian Bureau of Statistics. (2012b). *2071.0—Reflecting a nation: Stories from the 2011 census, 2012–2013—Cultural diversity in Australia*. Retrieved from http://www.abs.gov.au/ausstats/abs@.nsf/Latestproducts/2071.0MainFeatures902012%E2%80%932013.

Australian Bureau of Statistics. (2012c). *3101.0—Australian demographic statistics*. Retrieved from http://www.abs.gov.au/ausstats/abs@.nsf/mf/3101.0/.

Australian Government. (2013). *Guidelines on the recognition of sex and gender*. Barton: Commonwealth of Australia.

Baghramian, M. (2004). *Relativism*. London and New York: Routledge.

Barrett, J. (1998). Psychological and social funciton before and after phalloplasty. *International Journal of Transgenderism*, 2(1), 1–6.

Bhabha, H. (1990). *Nation and narration*. London: Routledge.

Brown, M., & Rownsley, C. A. (1996). *True selves: Understanding transsexualism for family, friends, co-workers and helping professionals*. San Francisco: Jossey-Bass.

Butler, J. (1990). *Gender trouble: Feminism and the subversion of identity*. London: Routledge.

Butler, J. (2004). *Undoing gender*. New York: Routledge.

Butler, J. (2005). *Giving an account of oneself.* New York: Fordham University Press.

Byne, W. (2014). Forty years after the removal of homosexuality from the DSM: Well on the way but not there yet. LGBT Health.

Califia, P. (1981). What is gay liberation? *Heresies, 3*(12), 30–34.

Callewaert, S. (2006). Bourdieu, critic of Foucault: The case of empirical social science against double-game-philosophy. *Theory, Culture & Society, 23*(6), 73–98.

T. Jones et al., *Female-to-Male (FtM) Transgender People's Experiences in Australia*, SpringerBriefs in Sociology, DOI 10.1007/978-3-319-13829-9

Carlson, D. L. (2005). Poststructuralism. In J. T. Sears (Ed.), *Youth, education, and sexualities: An international encyclopedia* (pp. 635–638). London: Greenwood Press.
Carroll, L. (2005). Intersex. In J. T. Sears (Ed.), *Youth, education and sexualities: An international encyclopedia* (Vol. 1: A–J, pp. 440–444). Westport, Connecticut: Greenwood Press.
Chauncey, G. (1989). Christian brotherhood or sexual perversion? Homosexual identities and the construction of sexual boundaries in the World War 1 era. In M. Duberman, M. Vicinus & G. Chauncey (Eds.), *Hidden from history: Reclaiming gay and lesbian past*. New York: Meridian.
Clark, T. C., Fleming, T., Bullen, P., Denny, S., Crengle, S., & Dyson, B., et al. (2013). *Youth'12 overview: The health and wellbeing of New Zealand secondary school students in 2012*. Auckland: New Zealand The University of Auckland.
Clements-Nolle, K., Marx, R., Guzman, R., & Katz, M. (2001). HIV prevalence, risk behaviours, health care use, and mental health status of transgender persons: Implications for public health intervention. *American Journal of Public Health, 91*(6), 915–921.
Clements-Nolle, K., Marx, R., & Katz, M. (2006). Attempted Suicide among transgender persons: The influence of gender-based discrimination and victimization. *Journal of Homosexuality, 51* (3), 53–69.
Collyer, F., & Heal, C. (2002). Patient satisfaction with sex re-assignment surgery in New South Wales. *Australia. Australian Journal of Primary Health, 8*(3), 9–19.
Couch, M., Pitts, M., Muclcare, H., Croy, S., Mitchell, A., & Patel, S. (2007). *Tranznation: A report on the health and wellbeing of transgendered people in Australia and New Zealand*. Melbourne: Australian Research Centre in Sex Health and Society.
De Cuypere, G., T'Sjoen, G., Beerten, R., Selvaggi, G., De Sutter, P., & Hoebeke, P. (2005). Sexual and physical health after sex reassignment surgery. *Archives of Sexual Behavior, 34*(6), 679–690.
Devor, A. (1997). *FTM: Female-to-male transsexuals in society*. Bloomington, IN: Indiana University Press.
Dibben, K. (2013). *School in backflip over transgender child's use of girls' toilet*. The Courier Mail,. Retrieved from http://www.couriermail.com.au/news/queensland/school-in-backflip-over-transgender-childs-use-of-girls-toilet/story-fnihsrf2-1226664333520.
Drescher, J. (2013). Controversies in gender diagnoses. LGBT. *Health, 1*(1), 9–13.
Edwards, J. W., Fisher, D. G., & Reynolds, G. L. (2007). Male-to-female transgender and transsexual clients of HIV service programs in Los Angeles county, California. *American Journal of Public Health, 97*(6), 1030–1033.
Equal Opportunity Act 1995. (2010). *VIC parliamentary counsel, 16/2010 congressional record*.
Equal Opportunity Act 1984. (2010). *Western Australia parliamentary counsel, 083 congressional record*.
Equal Opportunity Act 1984. (2010). SA parliamentary council (1.2.2010) *congressional record*.
Ehrensaft, D. (2011). *Gender born, gender made: Raising healthy gender-nonconforming children*. New York: Experiment.
Fausto-Sterling, A. (1993, March/April). The five sexes: Why male and female are not enough. *The Sciences, 33*(2), 20–24.
Fewster, S. (2013). *Family court permits orphaned girl 13 to undergo gender change. Herald Sun*. Retrieved from http://www.heraldsun.com.au/lifestyle/family-court-permits-orphaned-girl-13-to-undergo-gender-change/story-fni0d7e4-1226680759364.
Foucault, M. (1969). *The archeology of knowledge and the discourse on language*. New York: Pantheon Books.
Foucault, M. (1970). *The order of things*. New York: Pantheon.
Foucault, M. (1976). *The history of sexuality: The will to knowledge* (Vol. 1), Harmondsworth: Penguin Books.
Foucault, M. (1979). *Discipline and punish: The birth of the prison*. Harmondsworth: Penguin Books.
Foucault, M. (1980). *Power/knowledge*. New York: Pantheon.

Frank, M. (1989). *What is neostructuralism?* (Vol. 45). Minneapolis: University of Minnesota Press.

Freud, S. (1905). Three essays on the theory of sexuality. In J. Strachey (Ed.) (Trans. 1961). London: Penguin

Futterweit, W., & Deligdisch, L. (1986). Histopathological effects of exogenously administered testosterone in 19 female to male transsexuals. *Journal of Clinical Endocrinology and Metabolism, 62*(1), 16–21.

Gahan, L., & Jones, T. (2013). *Heaven Bent: Australian lesbian, gay, bisexual, transgender and intersex experiences of faith, religion and spirituality*. Melbourne: Clouds of Magellan.

Gahan, L., Jones, T., & Hillier, L. (2014). An unresolved journey: Religious Discourse and same-sex attracted and gender questioning young people. *The Social Scientific Study of Religion, 25* (1), 202–229.

Garber, M. (1992). *Vested interests: Cross-dressing and cultural anxiety*. New York and London: Routledge.

Grossman, A. H., & D'Augelli, A. R. (2006). Transgender youth: Invisible and vulnerable. *Journal of Homosexuality, 51*(1), 111–128.

Grossman, A. H., & D'Augelli, A. R. (2007). Transgender youth and life threatening behaviour. *Suicide and Life-Threatening Behaviour, 37*, 527–537.

Grossman, A. H., D'Augelli, A. R., Howell, T. J., & Hubbard, S. (2005). Parents' reactions to transgender youths' gender nonconforming expression and identity. *Journal of Gay & Lesbian Social Services, 18*(1), 3–16.

Grossman, A. H., D'Augelli, A. R., & Salter, N. P. (2006). Gender expression milestones, gender atypicality, victimization, and parents' responses. *Journal of GLBT Family Studies, 2*(1), 71–92.

Halberstam, J. (1998). *Female Masculinity*. Durham: Duke University Press.

Halberstam, J. (2012). Boys will be… Bois? Or, Transgender feminism and forgetful fish. In D. Richardson, J. McLaughlin & M. E. Casey (Eds.), *Intersections between feminist and queer theory* (pp. 97–115). New York: Palgrave MacMillan.

Haraldsen, I. R., & Dahl, A. A. (2000). Symptom profiles of gender dysphoric patients of transsexual type compared to patients with personality disorders and healthy adults. *Acta Psychiatrica Scandinavica, 102*, 276–281.

Harris, A., & Jones, T. (2014). Trans teacher experiences and the failure of visibility. In queer teachers, identity and performativity. In A. Harris & E. Gray (Eds.), *Queer Teachers, Identity and Performativity* (pp. 11–28). London: Palgrave Macmillan.

Heilmann, A. (2011). Gender and essentialism: Feminist debates in the twenty-first century. *Critical Quarterly, 53*(4), 78–89.

Hekman, S. (1999). Identity crises: Identity, identity politics, and beyond. *Critical Review of International Social and Political Philosophy, 2*(1), 3–26.

Hekman, S. (2008). Material bodies. In D. Welton (Ed.), *Body and flesh: A philosophical reader* (pp. 61–70). San Francisco, CA: Blackwell Publishing.

Hepp, U., Kraemer, B., Schnyder, U., Miller, N., & Delsignore, A. (2005). Psychiatric comorbidity in gender identity disorder. *Journal of Psychosomatic Research, 58*, 259–261.

Hillier, L., Jones, T., Monagle, M., Overton, N., Gahan, L., & Blackman, J., et al. (2010). *writing themselves in 3: The third national study on the sexual health and wellbeing of same-sex attracted and gender questioning young people*. Melbourne: Australian Research Centre in Sex, Health and Society.

Jagose, A. (1996). *Queer theory: An introduction*. New York: New York University Press.

Jeffreys, S. (1994). The Queer disappearance of lesbians: Sexuality in the academy. *Women's Studies International Forum, 17*(5), 459–472.

Jones, T. (2011a). Saving rhetorical children: Sexuality education discourses from conservative to post-modern. *Sex Education, 11*(4), 369–387.

Jones, T. (2011b). A sexuality education discourses framework: Conservative, liberal, critical and post-modern. *American Journal of Sexuality Education, 6*(2), 133–175.

Jones, T. (2012a). Data brief: The tasmanian education context. Hobart: Report submitted to Rodney Croome of the TGLRG and the Tasmanian Department of Education.

Jones, T. (2012b). *Minding Our GLBs & TIQs. A submission to the inquiry by the senate legal and constitutional affairs committee on the exposure draft of the human rights and anti-discrimination bill 2012*. Canberra: Australian Federal Parliament.

Jones, T. (2012c). Sexual subjects: GLBTIQ student subjectivities in Australian education policy. (PhD Doctoral thesis), La Trobe University, Melbourne.

Jones, T. (2013a). *Advance Australia fairer: A submission to the inquiry by the Senate legal and constitutional affairs committee on the sex discrimination amendment (sexual orientation, gender identity and intersex status) bill 2013*. Canberra: Australian Parliament.

Jones, T. (2013b). How sex education research methodologies frame GLBTIQ students. *Sex Education: Sexuality, Society and Learning, 13*(6), 687–701.

Jones, T. (2013c). *Understanding education policy: The 'four education orientations' framework*. Dordrecht Netherlands: Springer.

Jones, T., Gray, E., & Harris, A. (2014). GLBTIQ teachers in Australian education policy: protections, suspicions, and restrictions. *Sex Education: Sexuality, Society and Learning, 14*(3), 338–353.

Jones, T., & Hillier, L. (2012). Sexuality education school policy for GLBTIQ students. *Sex Education, 12*(4), 437–454.

Jones, T., & Hillier, L. (2013). Comparing trans-spectrum and same-sex attracted youth: Increased risks, increased activisms. *LGBT Youth, 10*(4), 287–307.

Karvelas, P. (2013). *Sex-swap kids being 'abused'*. The Australian. Retrieved from http://www.theaustralian.com.au/national-affairs/sex-swap-kids-being-abused/story-fn59niix-1226686573568.

Kenagy, G., & Hsieh, C. (2005). The risk less known: female-to-male transgender persons' vulnerability to HIV infection. *AIDS Care: Psychological and Socio-medical Aspects of AIDS/HIV, 17*(2), 195–207.

Kennedy, P. (2006). *The first man-made man*. New York: Bloomsbury.

Kissane, K. (2009, 04.05.09). *Court lets girl 17 remove breasts, the age*. Retrieved from http://www.theage.com.au/national/court-lets-girl-17-remove-breasts-20090503-arem.html?page=-1.

Kosciw, J., Greytak, E. A., Diaz, E. M., & Bartkiewicz, M. J. (2010). *The 2009 national school climate survey: the experiences of lesbian, gay, bisexual and transgender youth in our nation's schools*. New York: Gay, Lesbian and Straight Education Network.

Lankshear, C., & Knobel, M. (2000). Mapping postmodern literacies: A preliminary chart. In M. Yla-Kotola, J. Suoranta, & M. Kangas (Eds.), *The integrated media machine* (Vol. 2). Edita: Hameenlinna.

Lawrence, A. A. (2005). Sexuality before and after male to female sex reassignment surgery. *Archives of Sexual Behavior, 34*(2), 147–166.

Leitch, V., Cain, W., Finke, L., Johnson, B., McGowan, J., & Williams, J. (2001). *The Norton anthology of theory and criticism*. New York: Norton.

Lyotard, J.-F. (1984). The postmodern condition: A report on knowledge. In G. Bennington & B. Massumi Eds., (Trans.). Minneapolis: University of Minnesota Press.

McCredie, J. (2008, October 31). *Gender troubles* (p. 23). Australian Doctor.

McNeilage, A. (2013, 07.08.13). Sex education draft 'dreadful', The Sydney Morning Herald. Retrieved from http://www.smh.com.au/national/education/sex-education-draft-dreadful-20130806-2rdjd.html.

Michel, A., Mormont, C., & Legros, J. J. (2001). A pscyho-endocrinological overview of transexualism. *European Journal of Endocrinology, 145*(1), 365–376.

Miletic, D., & Browne, R. (2013). *Landmark ruling in hormone treatment case, The Age. Retrieved from* http://www.theage.com.au/victoria/landmark-ruling-in-hormone-treatment-case-20130801-2r23g.html.

Morton, D., & Zavarzadeh, M. (1991). Theory pedagogy politics: The crisis of "the subject" in the humanities. In D. Morton & M. Zavarzadeh (Eds.), *Theory/pedagogy/politics: Texts for change* (pp. 1–32). Urbana and Chicago: University of Illinois Press.

Nagoshi, J. L., & Brzury, S. I. (2010). Transgender Theory: Embodying Research and Practice. *Affilia: Journal of Women and Social Work, 25*(4), 431-443.
Newfield, E., Hart, S., Dibble, S., & Kohler, L. (2006). Female-to-male transgender quality of life. *Quality of Life Research, 15*(9), 1447–1457.
NSW Teachers Federation. (2011). *Gender, sexuality and identity*. Sydney: NSW Teachers Federation.
Pazos, S. (2000). Practice with Female-to-Male Transgendered Youth. *Journal of Gay & Lesbian Social Services, 10*(3–4), 65–82.
Pease, B., & Pease, A. (2003). *Why men don't listen and women can't read maps*. London: Orion Publishing Group.
Pitts, M., Smith, A., Mitchell, A., & Patel, S. (2006). *Private lives: A report on the health and wellbeing of GLBTI Australians*. Melbourne: Australian Research Centre in Sex, Health and Society, La Trobe University.
Plibersek, T., & McLucas, J. (2013). *All Gender Discrimination to be Removed from Medicare*. Canberra: Australian Government Department of Health and Ageing.
QLD Government. (2005). *Inclusive education statement*. Brisbane: Education Queensland Retrieved from http://www.education.qld.gov.au/studentservices/learning/docs/inclused statement2005.pdf.
Raymond, J. (1994). *The transsexual empire: The making of the she-male*. New York: Teacher's College Press.
Rehman, J., Lazer, S., Benet, A. E., Schaefer, L. C., & Melman, A. (1999). The reported sex and surgery satisfactions of 28 postoperative male-to-female transsexual patients. *Archives of Sexual Behavior, 28*(1), 71–89.
Robotham, J. (2012). *Child sex-change ruling fails to solve the confusion, The age*. Retrieved from http://www.theage.com.au/national/child-sexchange-ruling-fails-to-solve-the-confusion-20120210-1sjt6.html.
Roen, K. (2001). "Either/Or" and "Both/Neither": Discursive tensions in transgender politics. *Signs: Journal of Women in Culture and Society, 27*(2), 501–522.
Roen, K. (2011). The discursive and clinical production of trans youth: Gender variant youth who seek puberty suppression. *Psychology & Sexuality, 2*(1), 58–68.
Rowniak, S., Chesla, C., Rose, C. D., & Holzemer, W. L. (2011). Transmen: The HIV risk of gay identity. *AIDS Education and Prevention, 23*(1), 508–520.
Russell, S. T., Ryan, C., Toomey, R., Diaz, R. M., & Sanchez, J. (2011). Lesbian, gay, bisexual, and transgender adolescent school victimization: Implications for young adult health and adjustment. *Journal of School Health, 81*(5), 223–230.
SA Department for Education and Child Development. (2011). *Challenging homophobia in schools*. Melbourne: Government of South Australia.
Stark, J. (2009). *Transsexual takes to the footy field. The age*. Retrieved from http://www.theage.com.au/national/transsexual-takes-to-the-footy-field-20090606-bz7v.html.
Stephens, S. C., Bernstein, K. T., & Philip, S. S. (2011). Male to female and female to male transgender persons have different sexual risk behaviours yet similar rates of STDs and HIV. *AIDS and Behaviour, 15*(1), 683–686.
Stone, S. (1991). The empire strikes back: A posttranssexual manifesto. In J. Epstein & K. Straub (Eds.), *Body guards: The cultural politics of gender ambiguity* (pp. 280–304). New York: Routledge.
Stryker, S. (2008). *Transgender history*. Berkeley: Seal Press.
TAS Department of Education. (2012). *Guidelines for supporting sexual and gender diversity in schools and colleges*. Hobart: Tasmanian Government.
The Attorney-General for the Commonwealth v. "Kevin and Jennifer" and Human Rights and Equal Opportunity Commission (FamCA94 2003).
The Anti-Discrimination Act 1998. (2010). TAS *parliamentary counsel, 46 congressional record.*

The Senate Legal and Constitutional Affairs Legislation Committee. (2013). *Report on the sex discrimination amendment (sexual orientation, gender identity and intersex status) bill 2013 [provisions]*. Canberra: Parliament House.

Tiernan, S. (2009). It should not be so easy to construct a man: A history of female to male transsexuality in the journal Urania. In S. Tiernan & M. McAuliffe (Eds.), *Sapphists and Sexologists: Histories of Sexualities* (Vol. 2, pp. 56–70). Newcastle: Cambridge Scholars.

Transgender Victoria, A gender Agenda, OII Australia, NSW Gay & Lesbian Rights Lobby, & Victorian Gay and Lesbian Rights Lobby. (2013). *LGBTI organisations welcome new federal anti-discrimination protections*. Melbourne: Transgender Victoria Website.

Turner, A. (2008). *Pregnant trans man talks to Oprah. Pink news*. Retrieved from http://www.pinknews.co.uk/2008/04/03/pregnant-trans-man-talks-to-oprah/.

Tuttle, L. (1986). *Encylopedia of feminism*. London: Arrow Books.

UNESCO. (2009). *International technical guidance on sexuality education: An evidence-informed approach for schools, teachers and health educators (Vol. 1, The rationale for sexuality education)*. Paris: UNESCO Section on HIV and AIDS, Division for the Coordination of UN Priorities in Education, Education Sector.

UNESCO. (2011). *Rio statement on homophobic bullying and education for all*. Rio de Janiero, Brazil: UNESCO.

United Nations. (2012). *Born free and equal: Sexual orientation and gender identity in international human rights law*. New York and Geneva: United Nations Human Rights Office of the High Commissioner.

VIC Government. (2007). *Victorian government schools reference guide*. Melbourne: VIC Department of Education and Early Childhood Development Retrieved from http://www.education.vic.gov.au/management/governance/referenceguide/default.htm.

VIC Government. (2008). *Supporting sexual diversity in schools*. Melbourne: VIC Department of Education and Early Childhood Development Retrieved from http://www.eduweb.vic.gov.au/edulibrary/public/teachlearn/student/supportsexualdiversity.pdf.

VIC Government. (2009). *Gender identity*. Melbourne: Victorian Government Retrieved from http://www.education.vic.gov.au/hrweb/divequity/gender_id.htm.

WA Government. (2004). *Staff conduct perth: WA department of education and training*. Retrieved from http://policies.det.wa.edu.au/our_policies/ti_view?uid=aa7b64f5405351864b4ffa78280c72e9&iview=summary_view.

WA Government Department of Health and Department of Education, & Association of Independent Schools WA. (2002). *Growing and developing healthy relationships*. Perth: WA Department of Health Retrieved from http://www.public.health.wa.gov.au/2/233/2/school based_sex.pm.

Weininger, O. (1906). *Sex and character*. London: William Heinemann.

Yerke, A. F., & Mitchell, V. (2011). Am i man enough yet? A comparison of the body transition, self-labeling, and sexual orientation of two cohorts of female-to-male transsexuals. *International Journal of Transgenderism, 13*(2), 64–76.

Young, R. (1997). Comparative methodology and postmodern relativism. *International Review of Education, 43*(5), 497–505.

MIX
Papier aus verantwortungsvollen Quellen
Paper from responsible sources
FSC® C105338
FSC
www.fsc.org

If you have any concerns about our products,
you can contact us on
ProductSafety@springernature.com

In case Publisher is established outside the EU,
the EU authorized representative is:
Springer Nature Customer Service Center GmbH
Europaplatz 3, 69115 Heidelberg, Germany

Printed by Libri Plureos GmbH
in Hamburg, Germany